Raising a Happy Child

By the Editors of Time-Life Books

Alexandria, Virginia

TIME®
LIFE
BOOKS

Time-Life Books Inc.
is a wholly owned subsidiary of

Time Incorporated

FOUNDER: Henry R. Luce 1898-1967

Editor-in-Chief: Henry Anatole Grunwald
President: J. Richard Munro
Chairman of the Board: Ralph P. Davidson
Corporate Editor: Ray Cave
Group Vice President, Books:
Reginald K. Brack Jr.
Vice President, Books: George Artandi

Time-Life Books Inc.

EDITOR: George Constable
Director of Design: Louis Klein
Director of Editorial Resources:
Phyllis K. Wise
Acting Text Director: Ellen Phillips
Editorial Board: Russell B. Adams Jr., Dale M.
Brown, Roberta Conlan, Thomas H. Flaherty, Donia
Ann Steele, Rosalind Stubenberg, Kit van Tulleken,
Henry Woodhead
Director of Photography and Research:
John Conrad Weiser

PRESIDENT: Reginald K. Brack Jr.
Executive Vice Presidents: John M. Fahey Jr.,
Christopher T. Linen
Senior Vice Presidents: James L. Mercer, Leopoldo
Toralballa
Vice Presidents: Stephen L. Bair, Ralph J. Cuomo,
Juanita T. James, Hallett Johnson III, Robert H.
Smith, Paul R. Stewart
Director of Production Services:
Robert J. Passantino

Library of Congress Cataloguing in
Publication Data
Raising a happy child.
   (Successful parenting)
   Bibliography: p.
   Includes index.
   1. Child rearing. 2. Parent and child.
I. Time-Life Books. II. Series.
HQ769.R1685 1986   649'.1   86-5982
ISBN 0-8094-5913-2 (lib. bdg.)
ISBN 0-8094-5912-4

Successful Parenting

SERIES DIRECTOR: Donia Ann Steele
Deputy Editor: Jim Hicks
Series Administrator: Norma E. Shaw
Editorial Staff for *Raising a Happy Child:*
Designer: Raymond Ripper
Picture Editors: Neil Kagan (principal),
Jane Jordan
Text Editor: Robert A. Doyle
Staff Writer: Janet Cave
Researchers: Paula York-Soderlund (principal),
Patricia N. McKinney, Mark Moss
Assistant Designer: Cynthia T. Richardson
Copy Coordinator: Marfé Ferguson
Picture Coordinator: Bradley Hower
Editorial Assistant: Eileen Tansill

Special Contributors (text): Amy Goodwin Aldrich,
Lynne Bair, Megan Barnett, Elaine Blume, Sarah
Brash, Joan Britt, Pat Lewis Copeland, Betsy Frankel,
Lois Gilman, Louise Hedberg, Sandy Jones, Tom
Lewis, Brian McGinn, Wendy Murphy, Barbara
Palmer, Susan Perry, Brooke Stoddard,
David Thiemann.

Editorial Operations
Copy Chief: Diane Ullius
Editorial Operations: Caroline A. Boubin
(manager)
Production: Celia Beattie
Quality Control: James J. Cox (director)
Library: Louise D. Forstall

Correspondents: Elisabeth Kraemer-Singh (Bonn);
Dorothy Bacon (London); Maria Vincenza Aloisi
(Paris); Ann Natanson (Rome). Valuable assistance
was also provided by Christina Lieberman
(New York).

Second printing. Revised 1987. Printed in U.S.A.

Published simultaneously in Canada.
School and library distribution by
Silver Burdett Company, Morristown,
New Jersey 07960.

TIME-LIFE is a trademark of Time
Incorporated U.S.A.

Other Publications

MYSTERIES OF THE UNKNOWN
TIME FRAME
FIX IT YOURSELF
FITNESS, HEALTH & NUTRITION
HEALTHY HOME COOKING
UNDERSTANDING COMPUTERS
LIBRARY OF NATIONS
THE ENCHANTED WORLD
THE KODAK LIBRARY OF CREATIVE PHOTOGRAPHY
GREAT MEALS IN MINUTES
THE CIVIL WAR
PLANET EARTH
COLLECTOR'S LIBRARY OF THE CIVIL WAR
THE EPIC OF FLIGHT
THE GOOD COOK
WORLD WAR II
HOME REPAIR AND IMPROVEMENT
THE OLD WEST

*For information on and a full description
of any of the Time-Life Books series listed
above, please write:*
Reader Information
Time-Life Customer Service
P.O. Box C-32068
Richmond, Virginia 23261-2068
Or call:
1-800-621-7026

This volume is one of a series about raising children.

The Consultants

General Consultants

Dr. James L. Hatleberg, overall consultant for *Raising a Happy Child,* is Supervising Child Psychoanalyst at the Washington Psychoanalytic Institute and Clinical Assistant Professor in the Department of Psychiatry at the Georgetown University School of Medicine. Dr. Hatleberg serves on the executive council of the Washington Council of Child Psychiatry and currently practices adult and child psychoanalysis in Bethesda, Maryland.

Dr. Joseph Sparling, an educational psychologist, consulted on child development issues for the book. Dr. Sparling is a senior research investigator at the Frank Porter Graham Child Development Center of the University of North Carolina at Chapel Hill and is a lecturer in the School of Education at the university. He has developed toys and curriculum materials for young children, and his published work includes *Learningames for the First Three Years* and *Partners for Learning.*

Special Consultants

Dr. T. Berry Brazelton, a pediatrician and neonatologist, and **Lee McKenzie,** a pediatric nurse who works closely with him in studying the behavior of children, contributed to the section on early personality development. Dr. Brazelton is Chief of the Child Development Unit at The Children's Hospital, Boston, and Clinical Professor of Pediatrics at Harvard Medical School. The Brazelton Neonatal Behavioral Assessment Scale, which he developed, is used in hospitals worldwide. Dr. Brazelton is the author of *Infants and Mothers* and several other books on parent-child relationships, and he is the creator of the national television program *What Every Baby Knows.*

Dr. Joseph Campos, a professor of psychology at the University of Denver and a professor of clinical psychology at the University of Colorado Health Sciences Center, has done extensive research into early emotional development and the link between cognition and emotion in babies. Dr. Campos assisted in preparing the essay on how infants communicate their emotions.

Dr. Sylvia Feinburg, who helped to assemble the essay on children's art, is Chairman of the Eliot-Pearson Department of Child Study at Tufts University. Dr. Feinburg has taught art to children and adults. She has also trained art teachers and developed art education curricula in schools and day-care centers. She is a collector of children's art and writes and lectures widely on the subject of how children express themselves through drawing and painting.

Dr. Richard Ferber, who contributed to the section on sleep, is a pediatrician and the director of the Sleep Laboratory and the Center for Pediatric Sleep Disorders at The Children's Hospital, Boston. He is an instructor in neurology at Harvard Medical School and the author of *Solve Your Child's Sleep Problems.*

Dr. Stanley I. Greenspan assisted with the essay on children's emotional development, which is based on his recently published volume *First Feelings: Milestones in the Emotional Development of Your Baby and Child.* Dr. Greenspan is Clinical Professor of Child Health and Development at the George Washington University Medical School and an official in the Department of Health and Human Services, where he serves as Chief of the Infant and Child Development Services program for the Division of Maternal and Child Health. He practices psychiatry in the Washington, D.C., area.

Dr. Benjamin Siegel, a specialist on children's grieving, serves as a senior pediatrician in the Pediatric Primary Care Training Program at Boston City Hospital and directs medical-student education in pediatrics at the Boston University School of Medicine. Dr. Siegel contributed to the section on helping children cope with death.

The Photographer

Susie Fitzhugh, who photographed the cover picture, the developmental chart sequences and most of the remaining pictures in *Raising a Happy Child,* is a veteran child photographer who specializes in capturing candid portraits of youngsters in schools, hospitals and other real-life settings. Her work has appeared in many publications, including *The Family of Children, Exploring Photography* and the volume *Photographing Children* from the Life Library of Photography series.

Contents

4 Times of Special Stress 98

5 A Child's Development from Birth to Six 118

1
Foundations for a Happy Life

Childhood's earliest influences are the most enduring. By the end of your child's toddler years, much of her personality — the way she reacts to life's challenges, interacts with other people, feels about herself — will already have taken shape. If you are like most parents, you realize all too keenly that the chief architects of this emotional blueprint are none other than you and your spouse. And you worry about doing the correct things in your child's formative years.

But parenthood requires no special expertise, no esoteric skills. Mothers and fathers have been raising children more or less successfully for thousands of years. Most have done so without benefit of book learning or the advantages of educational toys, designer overalls and prestigious preschools. The only advantages that impress babies and toddlers, anyway, are the home-grown assets of parental patience, humor, understanding and love. In fact, experts agree, what contributes most to a child's future happiness is the unstinting love of his parents — and the knowledge that he is loved. You convey this not only by affectionate words and hugs, but also in the way you deal with your little one's everyday needs and concerns. It comes across in so small a matter as a busy mother's taking the time to stop, look and listen to her fledgling conversationalist, rather than just cocking one ear while bustling about her chores.

Most heartening of all, these expert-endorsed child-rearing techniques — which of course boil down to recognizing and accepting your child for the individual he is, loving him and letting him know that you love him — are within the reach of every parent, every day. That is what this book is about.

What Is a Happy Child?

A photograph album of your happy child should contain more than a collection of smiling faces captured on film at birthday parties and beach outings. Laughter and joy are the most obvious ways that a child expresses happiness, to be sure, but in its fullest sense happiness embraces a number of very different, sometimes conflicting qualities. To be complete, your album might include pictures of your 18-month-old refusing to put on his socks, your three-year-old looking forlorn as a balloon sails off into blue skies, your kindergartner's exasperation when the new bike proves difficult to master. The reigning moods of those pictures would be defiance, disappointment, frustration — which many parents consider negative or unacceptable. But the very fact that your child exhibits such feelings shows that he possesses their positive counterparts of assertiveness, pleasure and ambition. The ability to experience a full range of emotions, in fact, is in itself a sign of healthy adjustment. Far worse to have a child who is conditioned to act completely docile and deferent toward others, aloof in company, apathetic about new adventures, dispassionate when things do not work out as planned. This is the very antithesis of a happy child.

The happy baby

Although it may seem hard to believe, a crying baby is not necessarily an unhappy child. Infants cry for many reasons: fatigue, hunger, wet diapers, uncomfortable gas bubbles, too much stimulation or perhaps just boredom. Crying is the way babies let the world know of their feelings and needs. Parents must look beyond this noisy form of communication for signs of good emotional adjustment. One of the most important — in childhood and throughout adult life — is the capacity to give and receive affection and love. Your baby shows the beginnings of this art quite early. You can see it in the enraptured gazes she fixes on your face, and in her delighted smiles, kicks and coos as you play together.

Cuddling and clinging to her parents is another promising sign: Here the baby is exhibiting her dependency, showing that she trusts these all-important people in her life and feels safe with them. It is by having her needs met promptly and reliably when she is a helpless infant that the child in time gains the security she needs to venture forth on her own.

A happy baby will also display a healthy curiosity and interest in her surroundings. Notice how she reaches for toys in her crib, explores the wonders of your hair and ears, watches your every move with fascination. Involvement with people and events around her will be her primary method of learning, and another enduring source of pleasure throughout her lifetime.

The happy toddler

Your child will grow into toddlerhood carrying with him the curiosity and the cuddly qualities he developed as a baby. But the distinguishing feature of these years is his vacillation between the old dependency of babyhood and a new drive for independence. Children now become more consciously attached than ever to their parents, but at the same time a paradoxical event occurs: They learn to crawl and then to walk, gaining the locomotion to move away from the objects of their affection. This is usually the source of some short-term anxiety, but it is also crucial to the child's long-term happiness.

Watch as your child crawls or toddles boldly away from you and into the dining room, where he peeks under the table, grabs a bit of dust and wiggles the leg of a chair. Suddenly, something reminds him of you and, looking up in surprise, he either cries or scoots back to your side. Eventually he will gain more confidence and move more comfortably between his need for freedom and his desire for security. With the toddler's newfound mobility, curiosity flowers into rampant adventurousness. The happy child at this stage is into everything, asserting himself in exploring and testing, discovering new things every day. One thing he discovers quickly is that there are limits on his ramblings, which invariably produces some friction. His moods are mercurial, shifting from laughter to a tantrum and back to smiles within an hour. And most toddlers go through the period of ardent protest known as the "terrible twos." Considered from the long view, however, his barrage of "no" is really more assertive than negative. He is simply claiming his freedom to choose, while you stand by with your regulations. Gradually he comes to accept your authority, even to welcome it. Soon he will learn to set his own limits — another mark of the truly happy child.

The preschool years and beyond

Snapshots of your older child would show extraordinary eagerness to branch out in many directions at once. The preschooler's independence is rapidly turning into self-sufficiency, though frustration is evident when she bungles the knots on her shoes or reads the wrong time from the big and little hands of the clock. The confidence she will gain by succeeding on her own at these tasks, by solving her own problems, is another key factor in her present and future happiness. Experiencing frustrations and setbacks will teach her about life's realities, and weathering strife-filled episodes at home will help her see that the loving bond with her parents remains firm and unbroken, no matter what.

The ties of affection and trust established in her infant and toddler years will now blossom, too, into a host of social skills — a generosity of spirit, cooperative attitude, and consideration for other people's feelings — that will win her a welcome place in the society of her peers.

You will see your child's curiosity and adventurousness now finding their greatest expression in the pleasures of make-believe, which she pursues intensely. In fact, a flourishing imagination is one of the clearest reflections of healthy development. Children use pretend play to experiment with what they see and feel. By lavishing affection on her doll one minute and becoming mock-aggravated with her the next, your child shows that she understands and feels comfortable expressing all kinds of feelings — an important dimension of emotional growth.

No recipe exists for the proper mix of behavioral ingredients, just an understanding that the blend will be complex and rich. If you have supplied a nourishing climate of unmitigated love, acceptance and appropriate limits, your child's emotions will range wide and run deep: You can take that as the surest sign that you have a happy child. •:•

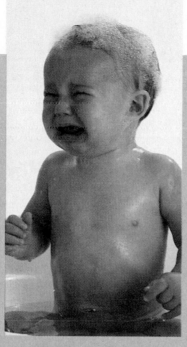

JOY over a playful accomplishment — here, waving a tickly feather — causes a baby to raise her cheeks and draw back the corners of her mouth, signaling that she wants the fun to continue.

DISTRESS at pain or discomfort, such as that caused here by an unwanted shampoo, elicits knitted brows, tightly-closed eyes and an open, square mouth.

SURPRISE provokes raised brows, wide eyes and a rounded mouth, which show shifted attention and readiness for a new activity.

A Language of Facial Expressions

To compensate for his physical helplessness, a newborn baby depends upon a remarkable set of survival tools — his built-in repertoire of emotional expressions. Until he can master his parents' language, they must master his: For months, emotional signals like those pictured here are the only means he has to communicate his basic needs and his reactions to the formidable world beyond his high chair and crib.

This wordless code representing joy, fear, surprise and other primal emotions that are present from the early weeks of life is the closest thing we know to a universal human language: Researchers have observed that infants of every culture, from middle-class America to the preliterate tribes of Borneo, use the same patterns of facial expressions, gestures and sounds to signal their feelings. And parents of every culture face the same task — to interpret their child's messages and respond in a way that ensures the little one's survival.

A baby's emotions work for her in two essential ways. Her positive expressions of joy, interest and surprise are like green traffic-lights: They tell her mother and father that she is enjoying the experience of the moment for the pleasure or information it is yielding, and encourage the parents to continue the stimulation. For example, when your baby sees an intriguing new toy, she will stare intently — a universal sign of interest that conveys to you the notion: "I like this. It is teaching me something. I want to go on exploring it."

On the other hand, your baby flashes negative emotions — distress, disgust, anger, fear and sadness — as red-light messages that something wrong must be remedied right away. Discomfort from gas pains, for instance, will invariably cause her to screw her eyes shut, furrow her brow, clench her fists, and whimper or cry — the universal distress call that summons your aid.

While parents are generally quick to notice and respond to the more gratifying expressions of their child's pleasure and curiosity, the subtler signs of negative emotions often go unrecognized until they have erupted in loud wails and tears. The most serious expression of all, however, is the silent face of sadness, an urgent message that distress signals have been ignored for so long that the baby has begun to withdraw.

By responding promptly to your infant's emotional expressions, both positive and negative, you are sending him an important message in return: He sees that his communication efforts can succeed, that his needs will be met, that his mother and father are creatures he can trust. This initial trust in a caring world, and the sense of security it provides, are carried deep within every happy, self-sufficient child.

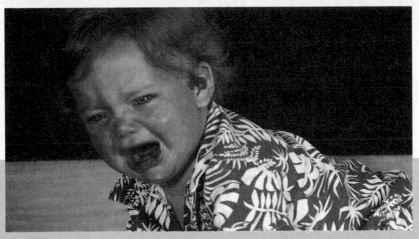

DISGUST over noxious tastes — here a sour pickle — is reflected by drawn brows, narrowed eyes, a lowered bottom lip and efforts to spit out the disliked substance.

ANGER in response to a frustration, such as the removal of a "no-no" from the baby's grasp, is shown by a furrowed brow, narrowed eyes and an angular, wailing mouth.

FEAR, mirrored in this crawling baby's lifted brow and eyelids, and tense, open mouth, signals that the child anticipates pain or danger and needs help.

INTEREST is manifested in a baby's intent, focused gaze, and shows a desire to continue exploring the object of attention — even if it is simply her own hand.

SADNESS, expressed by raised inner eyebrows and a drooping mouth, indicates that a baby is beginning to disengage and needs immediate attention.

Your Child's Emerging Personality

Only a generation ago, newborns were widely regarded as "blank slates," neutral little bundles of life whose personalities would be shaped solely by the way their parents raised them. It is true that the way you nurture your child has a major impact on his personality, but doctors now acknowledge what experienced mothers have known all along — that nature also plays an undeniable role. Children are born with many personal traits already in place — some no doubt inherited, others possibly caused by experiences in the womb or during childbirth. While it is not known exactly how these inborn characteristics come about, it is clear that they produce a surprising variety of infant behavior. Even identical twins, like the pair at right, can be physically indistinguishable and yet reveal distinctly different behavioral patterns and responses to the world. Fussy or calm, jumpy or cuddly, alert or aloof — such variations are quite normal and no cause for alarm.

At the same time, a child's individual nature should not simply be ignored. Babies with different personalities have different sets of rhythms, needs and preferences, and the very thing that delights one infant may bring woe to another. Some babies, for example, like to sit propped up amid the social bustle of the kitchen or the family room, while others need more sedate surroundings and far less stimulation. By recognizing and understanding your child's individual traits, you can provide the kind of care that will help him to thrive.

Clues to personality

There are many ways you can size up your baby's personality: She will reveal her likes and dislikes in almost everything she does. Experts in child development evaluate temperament by observing a child's responses in key areas of behavior. You can do the same by noting your own baby's reactions to such everyday activities as feeding, bathing and play. As you consider the following questions, think about possible adjustments to your routine that might make life easier for everyone.

First, does your infant adhere to a set schedule? After the settling-in period following birth, which may take as much as four months, some babies seem to develop built-in alarm clocks. They eat and sleep at roughly the same times each day. They have regular bowel movements and predictable times when they are either alert and playful or fussy and irritable. Other babies operate on no apparent schedule at all. One day this type of baby will sleep for so long that she has to be roused for feeding; the next day she will barely settle down for a nap at all. Parents of a child this unpredictable should keep their plans flexible.

How strongly does your baby show her feelings? If she is hungry or wet, does she cry loudly, flailing and kicking her arms and legs? Or does she fuss mildly at first to try to get your attention, only gradually intensifying her appeal if you do not respond at once? The less demonstrative the baby, the more alert you will need to be to her signals.

Another indicator of temperament is the way a baby typically reacts to new experiences. Does your child make his preferences immediately known, taking the first spoonful of cereal, considering its taste, then straining for the next bite? If he spits out the first mouthful, will he try

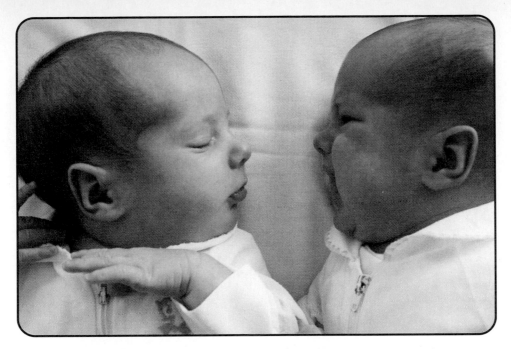

the new food again later on and eventually decide that he likes it? With some children, patience and persistence are needed when it comes to introducing unfamiliar people, places and things.

How much stimulation does your infant tolerate? Some children love being in a roomful of people, or watching the passing scene while out for a stroller ride. Others prefer to survey the sky or their own hands, and are unsettled by too much clamor. Parents will need to seek out quiet, unpressured activities for a child who is easily overstimulated.

Finally, what is your child's general mood and level of activity when she is alert and comfortable? Does she playfully kick, examine the mobile over her crib and listen intently to music playing in the next room? Or does she actively kick and squirm, propelling herself around the crib and then fussing when she gets stuck in a corner? You will surely have to interrupt what you are doing more frequently to keep a very active child composed and entertained. More often than not, the answers to the above questions will show some kind of consistent pattern of behavior; this pattern is what is meant by the term "personality." Most experts agree that babies fall roughly into one of three or four basic temperamental types; one expert's gallery of infant personality styles is described on pages 16 and 17.

Nature versus nurture Because a child does not grow up in a vacuum, his personality and ability to cope with the world ultimately embrace many more qualities than those he is born with. As he grows, his character develops and changes as a result of the people he lives with, the environment that surrounds him and the experiences he accumulates along the way. The largest personal influence will be that of his parents, whose habits and attitudes he will inevitably emulate. If the child has siblings, they also play a role in shaping his personality. And later on — around the age of six — peer influence and schooling may contribute to the pattern. But in early childhood, the predominant influences are in the home.

The "nature versus nurture" debate — over the issue of how much of a child's personality is dictated by nature and how much is absorbed from his environment — has been carried on for centuries and still seems far from settled. It is clear, however, that both factors are involved in most aspects of development. Researchers find it impossible to tell whether certain traits — such as a tendency toward aggression — are predominantly inbred or acquired. Other traits seem obviously determined by one influence more than the other. A tendency to be either calm or easily excitable, for example, seems to be chiefly hereditary, while a quality such as generosity appears to be most strongly influenced by the child's environment. In any event, it is a mistake to assume that the temperament an infant exhibits in his first months is permanent. A quiet, watchful child may indeed grow up to be a shy, conservative adult. However, given a certain pattern of interaction over the years with his parents and siblings, teachers and playmates, he could also turn out to be an outgoing and inquisitive grownup. In short, there is no way to predict with any certainty how your child's personality will turn out: Too many variables affect it. The important thing to keep in mind is that you, as parents, are chief among those variables.

Parental influences   The most profound way that you affect your child's personality is probably the least intentional or premeditated: It comes as a by-product of your normal interaction with the child in everyday activities. It is only natural for a youngster to do things as she sees them done by those who are closest to her; in essence, your child is busy every day integrating your attitudes and values into her own personality. And because a child's personality is a combination of many things — her view of herself, her approach to problems, her attitudes toward others, her values, and the way she reacts to frustrations and successes — almost anything that happens in the course of a day can add to the sum.

As your child moves from infancy into toddlerhood, you begin to teach her socially acceptable ways to behave so she can take her place in the larger world outside your home. The socialization process has a significant influence on her personality. You encourage her to be sensitive to the feelings of others, for example, or to be unselfish in play. The most direct way that you do this is by rewarding the behavior you like and punishing unacceptable behavior. But children learn much more by simply observing how their parents behave in social situations. A little girl, identifying strongly with her mother and her mother's emotions, will probably be overheard repeating the same expressions of loving concern to her playmates and dolls that her mother uses with her — or the same displays of sharp impatience, if that is the case.

In addition to influencing attitudes in such areas as dependency and self-reliance, fearfulness and aggressiveness, and in the formation of conscience, you also shape your child's attitudes toward behavior that is appropriate for his or her particular sex. The question of attributing certain personality traits to a baby's gender is another issue that has been fiercely debated for years, but researchers have in fact found very few biologically determined behavioral differences between male and female babies. Studies indicate that girls tend to be a little more watchful and able to concentrate for longer periods, while boys are slightly more restless and more inclined toward physical activity. But even these subtle differences have to be reinforced if they are to last.

Many parents do reinforce gender differences, in ways that are often quite unintentional. They may cuddle a girl more often than they would a boy, for example. Or they may roughhouse with a boy but play quietly with a girl. Because the socialization process does much to determine the child's attitudes toward sex-appropriate behavior, you have a clear opportunity to influence your child's outlook and personality in this regard *(pages 72-75)*. The way you proceed will in the end depend on your own views of masculinity and femininity — how you feel toward the traditional stereotypes of the tomboy and the sissy.

The role of siblings

Children often first learn about loyalty and responsibility by interacting with their siblings. Not many children will watch a younger brother or sister being taunted by playmates without rising to the defense. Children also become practiced in competitiveness and domination by battling with older and younger children in the family. Even this tiresome bickering seems to yield desirable side effects in terms of a child's personality. She learns how to moderate her feelings of jealousy and share an adult's attention, how to be flexible and to compromise in play — all necessary skills for a school-bound child.

The sex of a child's siblings and her birth order in the family also affect personality. Researchers have observed that girls with brothers, particularly older brothers, will often become more ambitious and aggressive than girls with sisters. Boys with older sisters tend to be less aggressive than boys with older brothers. And all children who grow up in a family with older brothers tend to be more physically active.

Studies have also shown that the oldest child in a family is likely to excel in areas deemed most important by the parents — getting good grades in school, for example — and may work harder to solve problems. This may be due to the exclusive relationship the child has with her parents until a sibling is born, and to the high expectations the parents typically have for their firstborn child. Later-born children, whose parents are more experienced and usually more relaxed in child-rearing, tend to adopt less demanding standards for themselves. A family's younger children tend to be less cautious than firstborns, as well.

The uniqueness of every child

The most important aspect of your child's developing personality, however, is its utter individuality. Children have the right to be themselves, regardless of what their parents may have hoped them to be. A parent's deliberate effort to impose direction on a child's personality will be futile, in any case, if it runs counter to the combined shaping forces of nature and experience. It is unlikely that any amount of pressuring will transform a quiet, contemplative child into the star athlete of his father's daydreams, or a restless, energetic youngster into a classical scholar. Be sensitive instead, to your child's particular way of responding to the world, and you will help him find the confidence he needs to develop his own personality and talents to the fullest. •:•

An Expert's View

Basic Types of Infant Temperament

It is nearly impossible to define what constitutes "normal behavior" for a baby. Every parent-to-be has visions of a cuddly, devoted infant who, though fussy at times, is generally wide-eyed and smiling. But in fact, the spectrum of normal behavior can be quite broad, and the reality quite surprising for parents. In my 35 years of pediatric practice, I have had the opportunity to talk with many parents and observe many babies. During these encounters, I discovered over and over that when parents were faced with a child whose temperament was completely different from their own, or from what they had expected it to be, they needed reassurance that their baby's behavior fell within the acceptable range.

Described here are behavioral profiles of three infants at the age of two months — the time at which many babies settle into a routine. While their personalities differ in many ways, all three are healthy and very "normal." The first, I call the average baby: This child is generally alert, comfortable and content. The second, the quiet baby, tends to be watchful and subdued. And the third, the active baby, is a tiny dynamo, usually in constant motion. When judged by their responses to routine care and handling, most babies seem to fall into one of these three basic temperamental types.

If you wish to determine your own child's temperamental style for comparison, simply observe him carefully during your everyday activities and note his general mood and reactions. Your baby may fall squarely into one of the three patterns outlined here or may combine traits from all three into a hybrid style all his own.

A parent who is unprepared to deal with a particularly active or quiet baby will at times feel frazzled and weary, or guilty and inadequate. Different children elicit different responses from their parents, and it is quite likely that preconceived notions of child rearing will crumble when put to the test. The thought to keep uppermost in mind is that each child, regardless of general personality type, is in the end an individual, with a unique mix of weaknesses and strengths. Accepting your child as such, appreciating and encouraging positive qualities as you understand and help the youngster cope with shortcomings, can be as enriching an experience for you as it is for your child.

The Average Baby

The parents of an average baby will consider themselves lucky indeed. This baby typically tunes in with interest and pleasure to the world around her and often welcomes new experiences. Adhering to a fairly regular feeding schedule, the average baby will usually begin to whimper and stir in her crib about half an hour before her accustomed mealtime; gradually she will build up to a strong cry to announce her hunger. This baby most often nurses quietly and steadily. When she has finished sucking and feels full and content, she is usually awake and quite alert. If placed in her crib or propped in a sitting position, the infant will observe her surroundings — staring at a beam of light coming through a window, or watching a fluttering curtain. When approached by parents or siblings for play, the baby usually responds by smiling and cycling her arms and legs.

As well as regular feeding times, this baby may have regular fussing periods, most often before bedtime. But the average baby is fairly adept at finding ways to soothe herself if attention is not immediately available. She may suck on her fist, turn onto her side, find a colorful toy or stuffed animal to watch, or suck on her fingers to reproduce the pleasant sensations of feeding. These fussing times can be trying, especially for parents who have only a limited amount of evening time to play with their child. But an average baby is basically even-tempered, and in return for the care and stimulation you give her, she will reward you with gratifying smiles, gurgles, and playful kicks.

The Quiet Baby

Quiet babies are generally wide-eyed, reticent children who approach life cautiously. They need time to warm up to new places, new people and new experiences. In raising a child with this temperament, you will need to be patient and encouraging as your baby adapts to changing situations at his own pace. A quiet baby sleeps much of the time but will usually wake at regular intervals for feeding. He may lie quietly in his crib, waiting for you to come to him, or he may whimper or cry softly to relay his hunger. The quiet baby relishes feeding, nursing slowly and steadily, and, at times, for an excessive period. This tendency to suck too long may cause the infant to spit up.

During the alert period after eating, the quiet baby may be relatively inactive, but he is keenly observing the things around him. He concentrates on watching each figure constituting his mobile, and stares intently at his fingers as he moves them toward his mouth. If interrupted by parents or siblings for gentle play, the infant may smile and respond. But stimulation can quickly become overwhelming for a quiet baby, and when it does he will retreat, turning away to block out the intrusion.

This child does not usually fuss in the evenings, but tends to wake up for a night feeding beyond the point when most infants are sleeping through the night. This may be due to the child's lack of motor activity during the day; he is not sufficiently tired to sleep all through the night. Eventually, however, by lengthening the time between feedings, you should be able to change this pattern.

Slow responses or a low level of feedback from an infant can be disappointing and discouraging for parents, who may blame themselves for their child's seeming lack of progress. They may assume that their child doesn't really need them — but actually the opposite is true. Quiet children need even more attention from parents to help stimulate their development. The key is to gear the stimulation to the child's level of coping with it. Ultimately you will find that a quiet baby can be as rewarding to raise as an outgoing child. More patience may be required to draw him out, but it is satisfying to know that each step he takes, each milestone he achieves, is one you have reached together.

The Active Baby

A whirlwind of activity frequently surrounds the active baby. This infant tends to be restless and easily distracted; her attention shifts rapidly from one object or activity to another. Like the quiet baby, the active child can be a lesson in patience for even the most tolerant of parents.

An active baby may or may not adhere to a regular feeding schedule, but when she is hungry you will know it from her loud, lusty cries; her crying is as intense as the rest of her. This infant cannot easily soothe herself, even for the few minutes she must wait while you prepare to nurse her. An active child usually eats quickly and with gusto, but her attention may be easily diverted by other activities taking place in the room where she is feeding.

When an active child is awake, her arms and legs are usually cycling like windmills. During play with parents or siblings, she smiles, gurgles, twists and kicks in response. But she also becomes easily overwrought by too much stimulation, and tears may come on with lightning speed. Her constant physical activity, in fact, can prevent this infant from making calm observations of sights and sounds as quieter babies do. The active child may have to develop special methods of slowing herself down — sucking on her hand or thumb, for instance — before she is able to focus her attention on an object or person nearby.

Active babies tend to have fussy periods before each nap and before bedtime, and they frequently resist their parents' attempts to soothe them by walking or rocking. They are usually light sleepers, rousing often during the night to whimper and move around in the crib, though most often they do fall back to sleep on their own. As the parent of an active baby you may spend much of your day simply trying to keep up with your infant, who will demand a great deal of attention. You may feel guilty about not being able to comfort her during fussy times, and even become desperate in your attempts to do so. If so, rest assured that the best you can usually do with an active baby is to maintain your patience, try to keep stimulation at a level she can manage, and learn to enjoy her freewheeling approach to life. It can be tense and exhausting, but also exhilarating, to witness the vitality of your energetic child.

— T. Berry Brazelton, M.D.
Director, Child Development Unit
The Children's Hospital, Boston

The Challenges of Parenthood

The individuals who will have the greatest influence on your child's emotional development — the ones who are most likely to determine how happy she will be, how she feels about herself, how well she copes with problems — are those whom child-care authorities call the "primary caregivers." Naturally, you will want to know as much as possible about these people. You may feel you know all about them already, since one of them is you, and the other is probably your spouse. But you should get acquainted with yourself anew, in your role as a parent, because becoming a parent changes you. If parenthood enriches your life, it also makes it more complex, evoking in you a confusing array of desires and expectations, fears and convictions.

Some of these personal attributes — a belief that children should mind their elders, for instance — a parent may know well. Others, such as a deep-seated fear of losing personal freedom, have a way of remaining hidden from view until some event inadvertently summons them forth. Then they pop out unexpectedly, affecting whatever the parent is doing or saying. When this happens, it can come as a big and often unwelcome surprise. The forces that shape your parenting style have many different sources. They include beliefs your own parents passed on to you, other attitudes you embrace mainly because your parents rejected them, expectations instilled by the culture in which you live, the opinions of friends, secret worries and fears that most new parents have but do not talk about, your individual temperament and, not least, the personality of the child whose arrival turned you into a parent in the first place.

The dream versus reality

These influences can start working even before the baby gets here. Some couples, while declaring publicly that they would be equally happy with a child of either sex, secretly nurture a preference for a boy or a girl. And some of them are so disappointed if their wish is not realized that, despite their best efforts, they respond to the child less enthusiastically than they would have otherwise during the first few weeks, which are a crucial period in the baby's emotional development.

An even more typical instance of expectations clashing with reality is that of the new mother who has just spent nine months picturing herself in idyllic communion with a cooing, chubby-cheeked infant. Instead she is handed a howling creature whose ruddy, wizened face is not yet plumped out with baby fat, whose head has been squeezed into a strange, elongated shape by its passage through the birth canal, and who utterly ignores her attempts to comfort him. One mother

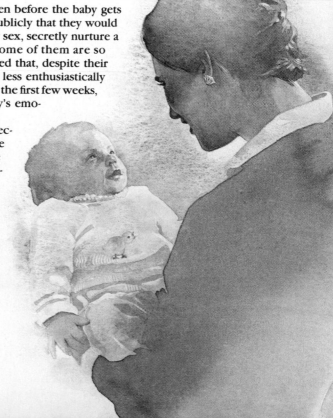

described her experience thus: "I was all prepared to love my son, but my good feelings were challenged from the start. He cried constantly, and no matter what I did to soothe him, nothing worked. I hate to say this, but I began to resent him and didn't like him very much during the first month or so."

If a parent who has such feelings refuses to admit that they exist, she may unwittingly hold back some of the warmth and positive response that her baby needs. It is better for her to acknowledge her own emotions, so she can work consciously to compensate for them. Mothers often find relief in discussing such misgivings frankly with a close friend, family member or minister who can help put their feelings into a new perspective. The important thing to do is find ways to keep giving the infant the physical and verbal affection he needs, even if doing so requires a good deal of effort. The child, who of course cannot control the way he looks or behaves, will in time repay these efforts a thousandfold.

The child within every parent

If you are like most parents, sooner or later you are bound to experience something like the following: Your child does something that annoys you, such as tearfully refusing to put on the new overalls that seemed to delight her so much in the store. Your normal, controlled response would be, perhaps, a reasoned explanation as to why we must wear the clothes that we buy. But instead you hear issuing forth from your mouth, in an eerily familiar tone and phrasing, a statement along the lines of "Is *this* my reward for all the nice things I do for you?" Or, "If you're going to cry, I might as well give you something to cry about." These words sound familiar because they echo those of your own parents — and perhaps of their parents, or even grandparents. Indeed, of all the baggage that men and women bring into parenthood, none is quite so heavy as what they carry from their own childhood days.

Whether you are conscious of it or not, your way of handling certain child-rearing challenges is apt to be strongly colored by the way your parents dealt with you in the same situations. Consider your reaction, for example, when your toddler talks back to you at the dinner table. If your parents were rigid disciplinarians who never let you get away with back talk, you might well consider it only natural to deal sternly with such behavior. Or you may react in the opposite fashion and be overly lenient with your youngster, as a kind of delayed protest against your own parents' strictness.

Sometimes these parental legacies can be a boon. Your ancestors, after all, did know a thing or two about bringing up children, and perhaps some of the things you do right as a parent are in your repertoire because your mother and father did them right when dealing with you. But occasionally the hang-overs from the past cause problems. When a father is too critical and demanding, for example, it may well be that his own father was overly critical of him when he was a child. Parents may even recognize a problem and its source, and nonetheless have difficulty getting it under control. One mother who knew she was mistreating her daughter pleaded with her doctor for help: "I'm hitting her and yelling at her — the same way my mother did."

In cases like this, when the problem is serious and not apt to go away on its own, parents owe it to themselves and their children to seek professional counseling. But parents who are endowed with milder family-linked traits are often able to deal with the issue directly through self-exploration. If you find yourself losing your temper unexpectedly or demonstrating some other kind of erratic behavior, stop and ask yourself, "Why did I do that?" Think back to your childhood to see if any relevant memory surfaces. It may even be worthwhile to make notes about what you recall of your own upbringing and the relationship you had with your parents. Were they too stern? Too indulgent? Were they generally cheerful? Were you? Talking your concerns over with your spouse or a friend who knows you well is another way of bringing some light to the problem. Your purpose in this exercise is not to fix blame or to find excuses for any faults you may perceive in yourself. It is to become aware of how your past affects the way you behave toward your own children, so that you can better control that behavior.

Those demanding expectations

Your mother and father were not the only sources of input into your parenting persona. Since first you served a dollies' tea party or watched a family situation-comedy on television, the whole cultural apparatus of the society you inhabit has been shaping your expectations about your performance as a parent — as well as your expectations about children. All these standards lay dormant within you until you had a baby of your own. Then, suddenly, they began a noisy clamor for satisfaction.

You are expected to be a wise and patient parent, ready with a smile and slow to anger. Your child may have fun faults, like not picking up her toys, but not any serious faults, such as being an obnoxious bully. And naturally you expect to love your children without qualification, and to enjoy their unceasing love in return. As experience will soon make clear, the gulf between expectation and reality can be wide. Here are some common expectations that inspire fear in many new parents, who wonder how they or their children will ever be able to measure up:

"If I make one mistake in the way I bring up my child, I will ruin her for life." Children are resilient. Consistent patterns of poor parenting can hurt them, but an occasional mistake does no harm.

"Having a baby should automatically ensure that my spouse and I improve our relationship." On the contrary, having a child frequently puts extra strain on a marriage, even a very stable one.

"My friend's baby already stands up" — or walks or talks or feeds himself — *"and mine doesn't, so my baby must be slow."* Every child

progresses at his own speed, so comparisons are counterproductive.

"As long as I am reasonable and logical in what I ask of my child, she will be compliant." Do not count on it. Children sometimes follow their own scripts, which may not agree with yours at all.

"If I get angry with my child, I am a bad parent." All parents occasionally are angry with their children. The object is to try to limit the occasions for frustration and anger, and to deal with them as coolly as possible when they do arise.

Parental anger

In fact, this last point is a source of much worry, because parents sometimes find themselves pushed into such rages by their youngster's behavior that they feel the urge to strike the child. Occasional impulses of this kind are natural and of no great consequence, as long as they do not become persistent — and as long as they are not actually carried out. Because young children look to their parents for safety and security, the sight of a mother or father becoming utterly unstrung and threatening to harm them can be very frightening.

The important rule to follow, therefore, is always to maintain control of yourself — both verbally and physically — in front of your child. Treat your violent reactions as a problem that is quite different and separate from your little one's behavior, and make sure to tackle the anger first, before you approach the child. The technique that works best for many parents is simply leaving the room for the moment and focusing on a cooling-down device, whether it is phoning a friend, splashing cold water on the face and wrists, or taking a brisk walk around the house. Or you may find that punching a pillow will help you release tension harmlessly. Once you have a hold on your feelings, you can return and deal more rationally with the events that set them off in the first place.

A meeting of personalities

Just as every child is born with a personality all his own, each parent has a distinct personality that shapes her needs and preferences, her moods and reactions to everyday events. And it is just as important that you be aware of your own temperament as it is for you to be aware of your child's, since the two will be existing in an intimate partnership. If your behavior modes happen to mesh easily, then you can enjoy each other's company without any particular effort on anybody's part.

But if your personalities are the sort of opposites that do not exactly attract — your baby skittish and cautious by nature, for example, and you a lively individual who loves a good romp — then one of you will have to make some adjustments. Needless to say, that person is you. If you find that your stimulating manner seems to make your infant tense, it may be that quieter play and gentler handling is required.

Keep in mind, however, that your child's personality can change with time. Do not make the mistake of assuming that you can never try enlivening his existence with your natural verve. Studies indicate, in fact, that children influence the way they are treated by their parents to a much greater extent than is commonly realized. Johnny appears to need a lot of protection, so his mother hovers over him extensively —

even though her natural inclination might be to give him more freedom and even though, after a while, he may very well crave that freedom.

Also bear in mind that you and your child may be so much alike that you need to make deliberate efforts to bring some balance into the picture. If you are both exceedingly placid, for instance, you and the baby might settle into a quiet, mutually unstimulating pattern of existence unless you make a point of drawing him out.

Balancing needs

It is a common error of parents to think that they must sacrifice all their own needs and desires to satisfy those of their children. Although, at the very beginning of parenthood, there is no getting around the fact that having a new baby creates biological and psychological demands that take precedence over previous commitments to yourself, it soon becomes apparent that your continued sanity depends on giving yourself a certain amount of consideration as well. You realize, too, that your proficiency as a parent is improved by a reasonable amount of self-indulgence. The frantic, frazzled mother simply is not as effective as one who sets aside a portion of time and attention for her own use.

There are some tricks for accomplishing this goal, despite the never-ending demands of motherhood. Some mothers use nursing time for self-reflection. The most valuable technique is to find an activity that benefits both mother and baby. Some mothers, for instance, discover that as long as they are down on the rug at their baby's level, he is content to let them read or sew while he crawls around exploring the room. The most obvious relief for the mother in a two-parent family is the father, who is not only capable of doing his share, but is actually depriving himself of many parenting pleasures if he does not.

When parents overdo it

Probably the most important lesson for a parent to learn is the principle of moderation. Everything that good parents naturally do for their children can easily be overdone. A good father, for example, certainly protects his child from danger; but if he is overzealous in doing so, she will never learn to protect herself from danger. A good mother wants to teach her child new skills, but there is a very fine line between teaching and interfering in a way that actually prevents the child from learning. Of course there will be times when you must override your youngster's wishes. There are very good reasons, for instance, for not letting her experiment with poking wires into electrical outlets. On the other hand, if she is making mud pies or building a tower with blocks, and she lets you know that she can do it perfectly well without your assistance, that is a good time for you to practice being a non-intrusive parent.

No one can set forth a pat formula that tells you how much guidance you should give your child in any particular case. But children are usually not shy about rejecting unwanted help, and yours will no doubt let you know when you have strayed over the line that separates "just enough" from "too much." In this matter, as in so many areas of parenting, you can learn a good deal about your effectiveness by simply watching and listening to your child. ❖

Parent to Parent

Keeping It in Perspective

The most successful parents are those who grow and change along with their offspring. Here, several mothers and fathers tell how they learned to focus on the important things in parenting — and laugh away the rest.

66 Jenny is really in a defiant stage now and we're having a lot of tantrums. When she wants to get even with her father and me, for instance, she picks up all her puzzles and flings them on the floor. It's very frustrating to me, because I feel that I need to be in control, to have a little order in my life. I have to give myself lectures about losing my cool. I tell myself to save the yelling for important things, like when she sticks her finger in the light socket, instead of when she puts on an orange shirt with purple pants. In the end you have to ask yourself what is more important. Do you want your child to remember that you yelled at her, or that there was love and gentle guidance? 99

66 As a single mother, I feel I've got special pressures. There is no one around to share day-to-day responsibilities. And some days I just don't want to be bothered. When you can make these little kids sit still or stay in their room, you get to feeling like you're throwing around power, like you can really tell them what to do. But then I realize I'm a lot like they are. I'm still figuring out what I need to do. They've just been my kids for three years, and I've only been a parent for three years. I'm still learning how to be a parent. I don't know everything. Sometimes I just laugh at how silly I must look, sitting up there with a stern look on my face about to hit somebody a quarter of my size. 99

66 Three-year-old Michael got hold of his mother's big powder puff and started powdering himself in our bedroom. He did his face, his tummy, his arms and his legs. Then he went to the full length mirror to admire himself. He obviously liked what he saw and powdered the mirror. Without missing a beat he then powdered the dresser, the doors and the wooden floors. I caught him as he headed toward the windows, and I was ready to really let him have it. But Michael got me first — and totally disarmed me. 'It's all right, Daddy,' he explained. 'I'm only dusting.' 99

66 When Gordon was five, I thought it would be great for him to take tap dancing. I even knew some of the kids signing up. But he just didn't want to do it. I kept pushing the idea until he looked at me and said 'Mom, did you ever want to take tap dancing?' And I told him yes, that I had when I was little. Then he said, 'Well, just stop wanting me to live the things that you didn't do.' How amazing it was, that the child realized what I was doing when I didn't even realize it myself. Children make a lot of sense if you talk with them and listen to them. 99

66 I really used to be a fanatic about the children's diet. A lot of times they didn't eat what I thought they should, and it drove me to distraction. By the time my third one came along, I realized that kids tend to eat what they need. So I hardly batted an eye when my oldest ate nothing but graham crackers for an entire week at the in-laws. Besides, by the time we got home he was so sick of graham crackers that he was eager to get back to regular meals. 99

66 My mother worried a lot about money, and I think I inherited that trait. There are times when I've swooped up the kids in a frenzy, dragged them to the bank and made them sit quietly while I talked to the bank officer about a bounced check. My son Tommy picked up on this in a telephone game he plays with his father. His dad will pretend to be somebody else when Tommy answers the phone, but Tommy always guesses who it is. This one time after Tommy figured it out, I overheard him ask his dad to call again and pretend he was someone from the bank demanding more money. I couldn't help laughing at his little joke on me — to think that a five-year-old could pick up on my anxiety like that. I've become a lot more aware of how it looks from the kids' point of view. Not that I'm cured of worrying about money, however. 99

66 Whenever Chris stuffs toilet paper down the toilet or does something else crazy like that, I think of the time when I was four or five. I thought orange was the most beautiful color in the world and I took a crayon and drew all over the family-room walls. I was so proud, I couldn't wait to show my parents. But when they came home they immediately overreacted, and made me clean it up, and just made me feel so ashamed. I always remember this when one of Chris's creative projects tries my patience. And if that doesn't work, I start my Lamaze breathing exercises and think, 'Don't get mad, he's only young once!' He looks just like me anyway, and it's awfully hard to get mad at someone who looks so much like me. 99

Building Self-Esteem

Most experts agree that a person's self-esteem — the measure of how he feels about himself — is the cornerstone of personal adjustment throughout life. A child begins early to seek answers to the fundamental questions "Am I lovable?" and "Am I worthwhile?" If the responses he receives from the people around him suggest that he is loved, wanted and capable, the chances are good that he will develop the same positive attitudes toward himself.

This sense of his own worth will find quiet expression in all aspects of his behavior. A child armed with high self-esteem will approach other people with trust, and view the world as a safe place where, most of the time, his emotional and physical needs will be satisfied. Like the "Little Engine That Could," he will face challenges with optimism, propelled by self-confidence to succeed as a winner in school, among his peers, and eventually in the countless contests of adult life. His opposite, on the other hand — the youngster who has been told in a thousand subtle ways that he is not always loved, not entirely wanted, not clever enough to succeed on his own — will in all likelihood be driven to take the low, slow road, risking little and gaining still less.

Not surprisingly, the child receives his first notions about his self-worth from his parents: They are his chief link to the external world throughout his early years, the mirrors in which he sees himself and his efforts reflected. A caring mother and father should examine the ways they handle their child and make sure their manner communicates positive messages and images — reflections that will enhance rather than undermine the child's sense of possibilities. It is also important for parents to broadcast positive messages about their own self-worth; a child learns best by example, and is far more likely to develop high self-esteem if he has grown-up models to follow.

Baby's first impressions

Child psychologists are convinced that a baby starts forming attitudes about herself while still in the cradle, in the process of forging bonds of love and trust with the person who cares for her. One mother, for

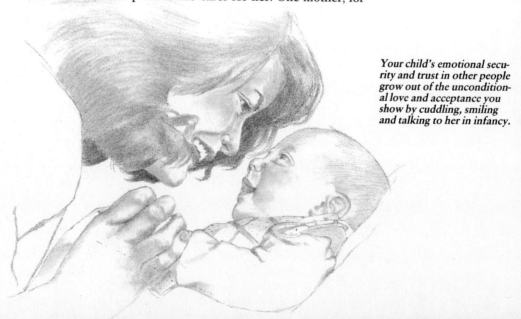

Your child's emotional security and trust in other people grow out of the unconditional love and acceptance you show by cuddling, smiling and talking to her in infancy.

example, may consistently convey positive estimates of her daughter's value — even in so mundane a situation as changing a diaper. As she makes the diaper switch, the mother gazes into her baby's eyes, smiling and chatting steadily, though she knows the child is still months away from understanding what the words mean. At the end of the task, she takes a few moments to play, cycling the baby's legs in the air and touching her toes together until she giggles. During this brief but potent exchange, the mother is saying to her child, "I love you unconditionally. You make me feel happy. Everything about you is fine with me."

Another mother, who cares no less about her child, goes about the same task in a more hurried, detached manner, viewing it as just an onerous job. There is a tightness in her muscles that the baby can feel as she washes and changes him, keeping her eye on a television show all the while. No sooner has she made the baby dry again than she sets him in an infant seat and turns away to clean up — with wrinkled nose and pursed lips that he will someday recognize as an expression of disapproval. Though this mother would not consciously send negative messages to her son, her actions translate something like this: "Changing you is a demeaning, smelly job. I love you, but only conditionally. There are things about you and your body that I resent." Her attitude inevitably colors the baby's developing feelings about himself.

Surround your baby with a stimulating environment to help her learn new skills. Show her how things work, so she sees that her actions can produce a response from the world around her.

A sense of mastery

If bonds of unconditional love are essential to emotional security, so too is a responsive environment — one that will allow the child to explore and learn, to try and succeed, and, in the process, to develop a sense of personal competence. Once again, the evidence suggests that experiences even in the early months of life can play a critical role in determining which youngsters will grow into expressive, self-assured, curious preschoolers and which ones will become timid, overcautious, and easily discouraged.

Experiencing the world favorably, as a place where one can express a need and get action in return, begins with something as basic as what happens when a baby feels hungry and begins to cry. The infant whose parent responds readily not only finds herself comforted with satisfying nourishment, but she also learns an important lesson: She has feelings that matter to others and can exercise some control over her circumstances. At the other extreme, the child who is left to cry and cry — perhaps because his parent fears that feeding him outside his normal schedule will spoil him — is being taught that his needs and actions are unimportant and that he cannot change his situation. Such a lesson can become a self-fulfilling prophecy, inclining the child as he grows older to passivity and a reluctance to take responsibility for his behavior.

Surroundings that stimulate

The physical environment you create for your infant is another tool in building his sense of self-esteem. Expose your child early to a variety of

Enjoying the physical affection and undivided attention of both parents in a rough-and-tumble play session makes your youngster feel that she is an important member of the family.

sights and sounds, including him as an observer in family events even though he is too young to participate. Provide him with age-appropriate playthings, either homemade or store-bought, that he can investigate through touch, taste, smell and sound. Choose toys that challenge him but that he can master with a little persistence.

When the baby is ready to crawl, give him a reasonable amount of freedom to explore physical space. If necessary, childproof one or more rooms where he can express his natural curiosity without your having to rein him in constantly. For those occasions when you must be out of sight for a few minutes, the indoor playpen and the backyard corral may be necessary. They are, however, no substitute for the rich experiences of footloose exploration.

Talking and touching

Oral communication is an essential ingredient in a stimulating environment. From your child's earliest days, make it a practice to talk to her while feeding, bathing and dressing her, for the sheer pleasure of it. Such interactions foster early language development, which in turn gives the child a powerful means of affecting her environment. The impersonal voices of television and radio do not create the same effect as your own; it is the direct, loving contact that encourages your youngster's early play with words. You can also read to her. At first she will simply enjoy the sound of your voice. Later you can look at picture books with her, naming the objects shown, helping her point her finger at them and praising her when she makes the right connections.

Touch is another powerful form of communication. Hugging, holding and playing pat-a-cake all express your loving acceptance while helping your child become familiar with the notion of her separate identity. But remember that whether you are talking to your baby eye-to-eye, showing her how something works or engaging in a family session of rough-house play on the carpet, it is vital to have frequent encounters in which your attention is undivided, focused on her alone. However brief such episodes may be, your total concentration during this time underscores your love for her, and tells her in a way she can understand how important and worthy a person she is.

A toddler's sense of self

Your unconditional love, the intellectual and physical stimulation you provide, your focused attention and your responsiveness continue to be very important when your baby moves on to the toddler stage. But now the child becomes an even more active participant in the relationship, projecting his own needs for self-expression and independence.

The two-year-old's celebrated testing behavior, for example, is a tool for building self-confidence. It is his way of saying that he now rejects infantile helplessness and wants to do some things on his own. He is looking for areas where you are willing to give a little ground. Even though he cannot negotiate these issues well in words and he is not entirely sure what he is equipped to do, he stands ready to challenge all limits, old and new. Rather than battle over trivial issues just to show who is in charge, let him test himself on tasks or activities that he has a reasonable chance of mastering with a minimum of supervision.

A chance to succeed Two of the activities your toddler will want to try his hand at are feeding and dressing himself. When he shows an inclination to take over on either, set standards for him that are within his reach, and then give him plenty of support and praise as he works toward improving his skills. For example, set him up for self-feeding in a situation where a bit of messiness will not matter, give him utensils that he can handle easily, and tactfully cut his food into bite-size pieces in advance.

Select clothes that are easy for him to put on and fasten. As he continues to grow and becomes more able to distinguish his belongings from those of others, foster his sense of ownership and responsbility by putting his name on his favorite things. Give him a special box or shelf where he alone can park his toys, and set aside a couple of low hooks on the closet door where he can keep his jackets and mittens. Don't expect perfect compliance at this age. Your youngster is sure to falter from time to time, but lots of positive reinforcement when he succeeds and a minimum of fuss when he fails will give him the opportunity he needs to master these and many other tasks.

Even if your toddler does not succeed completely when he tackles a new skill such as pouring from a pitcher, praising his attempt will foster his confidence and feelings of competence.

The freedom to fail Youngsters need to learn early that every new effort carries some risk of failure. Help your child to understand that disappointments and frustrations happen to everyone, children and grownups alike, and are nothing to be ashamed of. Let her know that making an honest effort to perform a task is in itself grounds for feeling proud, and express your confidence that she will succeed on the next try, or perhaps the time after that. Show her ways to approach a challenge if she is having trouble on her own. For

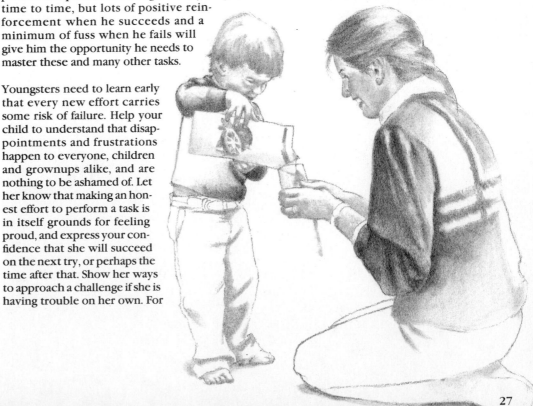

example, if your daughter returns with her toothbrush when you have asked her to bring her brush and comb, you could say: "Thank you for going to look. Let's go together, now, and find that brush and comb." In this way you focus on the process and the correct result, rather than on her performance and the mistake.

Decision making is another critical skill your youngster needs guidance in. To a young child, making choices can seem to be a life-or-death matter. Help demystify the process by giving your youngster opportunities to make simple choices in inconsequential matters. For example, you can invite your four-year-old to choose between two sweaters when you are shopping, or let her decide where to put the balloons for her sister's birthday party. Encourage her to think out loud about her reasons, so that she sees herself as a person who uses her head.

Teaching self-control

Your child's need to feel competent in practical matters is matched by his need to feel a growing sense of self-control in his behavior. Firm, consistent parental discipline is crucial: Neither rigid authoritarianism nor wishy-washy permissiveness prepares the child for the world he will function in. The first system gives all responsibility for behavior to the parents and leaves little or no room for the child to choose and experiment; the second turns all control over to the child without rehearsing him in the kinds of behavior the world will expect of him. What is needed is a style of discipline that falls somewhere between these two approaches. You will need to make clear to your child what you consider acceptable behavior. Explain that you think him capable of living up to these expectations and that you will correct him when he is off the mark. Be consistent in your expectations, so the child will understand the value you place on certain standards of behavior.

When your child breaks a rule, as this youngster has by using sharp scissors, you should accompany your correction with a positive alternative that will help him learn to discipline himself.

Transgressions should not be overlooked, but let your method of discipline be appropriate to the child's level of understanding. Never forget that making your child feel loved is the most important rule of discipline, and that the ultimate objective is for him to learn to discipline himself. When he does break the rules and needs correcting, focus your complaint on the troublesome act rather than on the child. For example, if your son willfully knocks down his friend's fortress of blocks, tell the spoiler that "Knocking over the fortress makes your friend feel sad," rather than "You were mean." In this way you make your point forcefully without attaching a negative label to your child.

At the same time, avoid too much descriptive praise. Statements such as "You're my perfect little angel" may actually undermine self-esteem by suggesting that you love the child for his good behavior rather than for himself. Children know, usually better than their parents, that they are not perfect angels; when a child hears this sort of praise he is likely to remember hidden misdeeds and fear his parents will love him less if these secrets are ever revealed. It is better to direct praise toward the child's accomplishments and to avoid characterizing his nature.

The gift of true listening

As her language skills flower, your toddler will also try out her competence as a talker. Not all of what she has to say will be interesting, and

Give your child the freedom to express his emotions, whatever they may be. Your attentive listening and non-judgmental attitude let him know that all his feelings are legitimate.

often she will want to talk when you are terribly busy. Nevertheless, it is vitally important to her feelings of self-worth that you set aside your duties and distractions and devote some period of time every day simply to listening to what she has to say. The same sorts of connections that were important when you played with her in her first months of life apply here: Show her that she has your full attention with eye contact, touching, and a hug when the spirit moves you. Treat her questions and opinions with respect; if you act as if they are silly, pointless or boring, she is likely to conclude that the same applies to her. Correct your youngster's misstatements only if you think wrong information could get her into difficulties, and be tolerant of a large measure of joyous fantasy and exaggeration.

When your child reveals her feelings about herself or others, let her talk freely as you listen carefully, showing that you truly understand by the things that you say in response. If your three-year-old tells you she feels like throwing the baby in the garbage can, you can acknowledge her feelings, her right to express them and your understanding by saying, "Wow — you must really be angry. What has the baby done now?" Though the child's feelings may disturb you at times, it is important that she feel free to express them without fear of admonishment or punishment. Otherwise, she will learn to feel guilty about her emotions and will probably stop sharing them with you.

If children are great talkers, they are also great listeners, and you should be careful not to make offhand comments that convey negative messages to your youngster about herself. A child who overhears her mother tell a neighbor that she is shy with strangers or a fussy eater can interpret such negative descriptions as permanent conditions that she is powerless to overcome. And a particularly sensitive child may even take a joking nickname such as "klutz" or "fatty" to heart and start playing the part in earnest.

To encourage positive, self-confident behavior on the part of your child you must, first of all, let her know you feel positive and confident that she is capable of succeeding. In the beginning, as new challenges present themselves, she will want to do well to please you. But in time, as your love nurtures her self-love and self-esteem, your child will be flying free — striving to please herself. This momentum, established through your thousands of everyday words and deeds during the early years, will carry her forward all the days of her life. ∴

A Child's Journey to Emotional Maturity

Of all nature's transformations, none is so dramatic as the blossoming of a human child in the first years of life. The newborn infant, expert only at suckling, sleeping and crying, evolves by kindergarten age into a loving, scheming, probing, teasing, feeling social being.

This journey toward emotional competence begins at the very moment of birth, when the baby emerges from the cushioned haven of the womb into a world of sudden, harsh sensation. There is blinding glare, a startling new temperature, the urgent pressure of hands giving care and oxygen abruptly pouring into untried lungs. The senses, for the moment, are the newborn's greatest torment — but they are also her only tools. Forever after, the world will thrust at her a torrent of sights, sounds, smells, tastes and tactile sensations. Tiny and helpless as she is, the infant faces the first great task of her life: She must learn to deal with the ceaseless stimulation of her senses, to use every sensory message as a lesson about her surroundings.

As you watch your child progress along this learning course over the years, you will see milestones of physical, verbal and intellectual growth glide by like exits on a well-marked highway. Signs of emotional progress are more difficult to detect. You may not even notice when your child first makes the connection between smiling and receiving affection in return, first mimics adult anger or uses a word to label some inner feeling. But these are critical steps in a passage to emotional understanding. Each new achievement paves the way to further progress. And, in large measure, the course of this emotional journey determines the kind of person the child will someday become.

The behaviors discussed on these pages have been noted by leading scholars in the field of child study, among them the developmental pioneers Erik Erikson and Jean Piaget. Although no one can say for sure what takes place within the mind of a baby or very young child, most experts believe that the child's emotional learning begins with a general interest in the world, an interest that first finds focus in attachment to a parent, then broadens into a need for ever-wider social interaction.

Expanding upon these principles through years of research and observation for the Department of Health and Human Services, child psychiatrist Stanley Greenspan has further theorized that a child's emotional maturity is built around certain key turning points, each one setting the stage for those that follow. Perhaps most important, Dr. Greenspan has described ways that parents can help nurture their child's unfolding emotional life.

In the developmental sequence pictured on these pages, the

Cradled in a doctor's hands (inset), the newborn girl looks shocked by her first impressions of the world. She is still linked to her mother by the umbilical cord, but she has filled her lungs with air, and her brain is receiving messages from all five senses. Newborns are thought to be very nearsighted, and this baby's first glimpses of the delivery room are probably a meaningless jumble of lights and shapes. For now, she may have to find comfort in other sensations, such as warmth on her skin or the sweet taste of mother's milk.

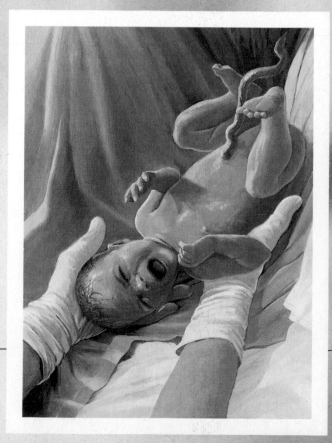

Now two months old, the infant shows an unmistakable fascination with her mother's face. The baby's vision has improved to a point where she can search her mother's eyes or study her smile, though perhaps she still cannot focus on the whole face at once. When the mother responds to her baby's interest with loving gazes, smiles and quiet words (inset), the baby smiles back and seems to hunger for ever more attention. Mother and child are in the process of forming a deep emotional bond.

pairings of large and small drawings are an artist's representation of the major milestones identified by Dr. Greenspan. The smaller picture of each pair shows an objective event in the child's daily life, and the larger one — viewed from the child's perspective — illustrates how that experience is believed to relate to the child's social and emotional growth. Some of Dr. Greenspan's suggestions for shepherding children through these stages of growth appear in the accompanying parents' role boxes. And parents, who know their children best, can find many more imaginative ways to encourage learning.

In the normal course of infant development outlined by Dr. Greenspan, after the baby recovers from the tumult of birth and settles into her new home, she spends her first few weeks finding ways to calm herself amid the rush of sensations that confronts her. This she seems to accomplish by focusing on sensations that she likes — perhaps the dependable sound of a ticking clock, the coolness of bedding pressed against her cheek, or simply the shifting patterns of light from the window by her crib. At the same time, the child is developing an interest in her strange new world. The taste of mother's milk, the warmth of the bath, the scent of a visitor's perfume — gradually she learns that such sensations explain the things around her. These two small skills work together for the child. She uses her senses to gain self-control in the face of a sometimes overwhelming environment; and by taking an interest in the world of sensations she learns new ways to be calm.

Each of these seemingly tiny steps forward is fundamental to future emotional growth. Certainly, the child's capacity to control her feelings and her readiness to regard the world with interest will be essential to any meaningful social or emotional exchange. In the short term, this mastery of the senses is a steppingstone to the child's next important stage — forming a first strong emotional bond.

Mother's bright red sweater, the texture of a fuzzy stuffed toy, the chatter of a sibling at play — any random discovery can attract attention during the first weeks of life. But soon this indiscriminate interest in the world begins to become more focused. During the second, third and fourth months, the child zeroes in on Mother. There is a growing sense that human contact is the most essential experience, the part of the landscape that can be counted upon to provide food and other comforts. Sometime between the fourth and eighth weeks of his life, your child finds a way to indicate his budding fascination.

One day, while he ponders your face, your child quite unexpectedly lights up in a smile. This first real sign of recognition

The Parents' Role

Draw your child into a loving relationship by engaging her in quiet, tender exchanges. Here are some suggestions to follow for courting your child's affection:

● Hold the baby securely in front of you where she can easily look at your face. While rocking the child in your arms, smile at her, cuddle her and make cooing sounds.

● Watch the baby's reactions. Does she return the smile and coo at you? Does the baby explore your face with her eyes or with her hands?

● As you woo the child, heed her attention span. Before she starts to get irritable, you should switch to a more physical, less intimate activity.

● If she fusses, soothe her, and then resume your play in calmer and more subtle ways.

● If the child seems unresponsive, try courting her in a more expansive and emotional style.

At six months of age, the child waves her arms and chirps out a stream of random sounds to show that there is something she wants (inset). When her mother responds to these overtures by handing her a toy, the girl learns a lesson in cause and effect: She sees that her actions elicit a response. Recognizing that she can have an impact on the people around her motivates the child to make conscious attempts to communicate.

can be mightily affecting; many parents remember these enraptured first smiles as vividly as their child's first steps. And in terms of the baby's emotional development, fascination with the human face and voice is truly a giant step forward.

The seeds of a new emotion have been planted, and it is up to you to help your child bring it to fruition. By responding to his smiles and showing him quiet love and affection, by talking to him and being his steady companion, you show your child that there is a rewarding side to life beyond the mere satisfaction of physical needs. You are, essentially, wooing your baby into human society. Over time, his fascination turns to love.

The importance of this first deep emotional relationship cannot be overstated, for it is from this primary human attachment that all subsequent social relationships flow. The infant has sampled the benefits of having an emotional partner, and at some point between two and 10 months, he will be ready for the next step of his journey: He will take the initiative in communicating with others.

During the middle months of her first year, the baby begins physically reaching out a hand or flagging her arms to show that there is something she wants. In company, she smiles, makes inexpert gestures and utters small sounds in an effort to elicit a response from those around her. When these overtures are answered — when someone smiles back or mimics her movements and haphazard noises — the child learns that she has the power to make something happen.

She has discovered a reason to communicate — a major leap forward on the path to emotional maturity. Exploring this exciting new reflex of cause and effect, the child sees that by stretching out her arm, she can sometimes get a toy in her hand. In the same manner, the child learns that by smiling and making a show of her joy, she has the ability to create happiness in her parents. The child discovers that her actions and her feelings can make a difference.

In her first nine months, a child developed a taste for the world; almost immediately, she sensed her need for people and formed a deep emotional bond with the person central to her care; the child's affection for her mother then broadened into a will to communicate, and — even though her tools of self-expression were minimal — she found she could provoke an emotional response. Now the child wants to communicate in many different ways. She is poised for an explosive burst of growth, both in her motor skills, which so far have been limited, and in her emotional repertoire.

When your child is somewhere between 10 and 18 months

The Parents' Role

By example and through frequent interaction with your infant, encourage him to communicate with you.

● Pay attention to the ways your child tries to express himself. Does he most often make sounds, gestures or facial expressions? Favor those same signals when you initiate an exchange.

● Respond appropriately to the baby's attempts to communicate. If he reaches for a toy, hand it to him. If he smiles, stop and smile back at him.

● Show him how to combine different communication skills. If he prefers to vocalize, play games such as peekaboo that include that skill as well as another.

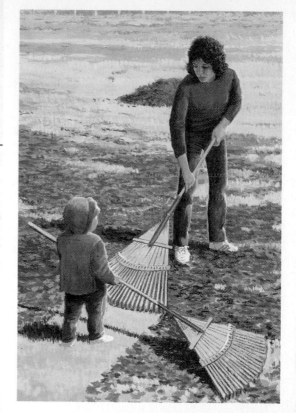

old, notes Dr. Greenspan, you will observe him stringing together sequences of actions. A one-year-old may race on all fours to greet his father at the door. He may pull himself to his feet by clutching at Daddy's pant legs and chortle when he is lifted for a hug. Your youngster is acting upon his understanding of cause and effect, learning to form patterns of behavior and to intermix actions with bits and pieces of emotion. These are the first signs of an ability to organize.

Previously, when your child got angry, it was a fleeting reaction that led nowhere. Now he may crawl over and bite the playmate who inspired his anger. He also shows his love more demonstrably, making a big show of bestowing hugs and kisses. When the toddler learns to pout, he has found a way to act out his disappointment and uses it to play for his parents' sympathy. A little later on, he shows the beginnings of pride. He wants you to notice when he stacks three blocks or pulls off his socks all by himself. All these developments are tokens of your child's first real sense of who he is.

This emerging sense of self is shaped as the child experiments with patterns of behavior. She is constantly watching, always trying to learn how things work. She leafs a dozen times through a magazine, empties the cupboard of all the pots and pans. She discovers that everything has a specific function: A rake scrapes up leaves, the telephone carries voices, the high chair holds her up where she can see her parents' eyes. All the while, the child is studying her parents' actions and finds that they have their functions as well. She begins to imitate adult behavior as a way of trying out the actions and emotions she observes, and in some cases, what starts as imitation becomes the real thing. With this new tool at her disposal, the child can initiate actions to get her needs met — tugging on the refrigerator door, for example, to show that she is thirsty and wants a drink of juice or milk.

As your child approaches a year and a half, you will notice him behaving in patterns that make emotional sense and are socially acceptable. If he gets caught in the middle when you scold his older brother, he may try to defend the older child with a hug or try to restore your good humor by laughing and flashing an unusually bright face. More and more, in this age of growing independence, he is striking out on his own, emerging as a unique individual with his own quirks and personality traits. You begin to get a reliable sense of the kind of person your youngster will be.

In the midst of all these changes, your child has started to speak a few words and seems to understand when Mommy has

Confident afoot at 18 months, the child is now freer to explore her surroundings and to imitate her mother's activities (inset). In a characteristic pattern, the toddler's mimicry of her mother's work with the rake leads her to focus on how the rake does its job. In this way, she comes to realize that the objects around her have specific functions. The child is beginning to piece together an organized view of the world.

The Parents' Role

Show your child organized ways to behave.

● Take the time to demonstrate how things work — such as how to flip the light switch and how to hold the phone.

● Help her carry an activity through several steps. If she is holding a ball, first show her how it bounces, then roll it back and forth, and then help her put the ball back in the toy box.

● Encourage your child's independence by allowing her to explore, but make limits known by your words and actions.

The Parents' Role

In conversation and play, help your child focus on the various impressions that he will need when he begins to form abstract ideas.

● Encourage him to analyze function: What is a cup for? Why do you wear shoes?

● Discuss the different roles that people play: What does Daddy do? Why does Mommy go to work? Who takes care of you when you get hurt?

● Focus on physical details: What color is the truck? Is the ladybug big or is it little?

to say "no." His capacity for social and emotional growth seems to unfold a little faster with each new day.

At some point shortly after the child reaches 18 months of age, she makes a revolutionary mental leap: She begins to form ideas in the abstract. This ability, coupled with a growth in language, makes possible a leap to the next higher emotional level. Now she can use her mind, rather than raw behavioral patterns, to satisfy her physical and psychological needs.

The child who has reached this conceptual milestone can search for a toy or stuffed animal that has been hidden from her sight in a playful game, because she is able to form a mental image of the hidden object. On a social or emotional level, the child can envision a person not present in the room or can recall an interaction with that person.

This newfound ability to create abstract ideas has its roots in the child's earlier discovery that objects have specific functions and perform certain tasks. The child saw that this lesson held true for people as well. Mother gives her food, puts on her clothes and can be counted on to hand her a toy; Father reads books and drives her in the car. Mother and Father also play a major role within the child's world of feelings. They laugh with her, respond to her love, and comfort her when she is upset. And by now the child is thoroughly familiar with the physical characteristics of her parents; after all, she first began to study their faces when she was about a month old.

Gradually the child brings all these separate impressions together. She links observations about the way her parents look and behave to the feelings and expectations they stir in her. In doing so, she creates a single mental image of her mother and of her father. The toddler has formed an idea that she can use.

This valuable emotional tool increases her self-sufficiency. Until this point, the child responded to emotions strictly on a behavioral level. As a very young infant she calmed herself by focusing on familiar sensations; later, when she was upset, she flailed out at what disturbed her, or she started to cry. But at this toddler stage, the child is starting to approach the world conceptually as well. She can comfort herself by conjuring a mental picture of a person she trusts and loves, or of pleasurable objects and experiences. Her feelings are translated into a mental image that tempers and guides her emotional expression. The child is beginning to understand how feelings and actions should mix and work together.

Using the new words she is learning, she labels her ideas with names. This allows her to plan more complex actions, combining two or more related ideas. At two and a half, for example, the

While the child's father serves breakfast, her mother is out of sight in the next room (inset), yet the two-year-old can visualize her mother joining them at the table. The capacity to summon mental images of her absent parents is a valuable new security device for the child. More than that, however, the ability to create and use ideas is crucial to her future emotional growth. The youngster must learn to express her feelings and needs through rational channels rather than continuing to rely solely on behavior.

At two and a half, the youngster has verbal skills that help her organize ideas and solve simple problems, such as how to get a teddy bear that is too high up to reach. By calling out for assistance, she shows that her idea of her mother includes, among other things, a person who has helped her in the past to reach things (inset). The appearance of language is the most obvious sign that a child has achieved the milestone of symbolic thought.

child spies a favorite toy that is up too high to reach. She calls out to mother, then points and says "want it" when mother arrives. The child has identified a need, formed an idea of the solution to that need, combined the idea with her concept of mother, then put her ideas into words. She has, in short, used her mind to solve a problem. When the child tells you she is scared, happy or mad, she is summarizing all that she has felt and observed about those emotions. With experience, her understanding will be greatly refined, but by the simple act of applying the correct label to her feelings, she has acquired a powerful tool for organizing her emotional life.

The use of language is the most obvious way that a child reveals newfound conceptual abilities. But different children arrive at this stage with different tools at their disposal. Some children first show their use of ideas through fantasies and pretend play. Earlier, the child learned that you draw with a crayon and drink from a cup. Now she makes these objects part of her make-believe games. Her toy bear sits with her in front of the coloring book and is allotted a share of the crayons. Later the child offers the bear a sip from her empty cup. She is showing the ability to use ideas. When the child lavishes care or affection on the toy animal, she has evidently abstracted her own need for care and formed an idea about love.

Some children communicate ideas quite well with gestures before their language skills bloom. At two and a half, a child might tug at Mother's blouse and point to the baby, thereby telling her that it is time for baby brother to nurse. Working only with gestures, the child shows concern for the baby.

Another way that your child might first use ideas is through the spatial patterns that he devises when playing with his toys. A child who organizes a long, straight line of toy cars clearly has a preconceived mental picture that gives structure to his game. When the child opens a "gate" in a wall of blocks and drives a car through, he is demonstrating yet another idea.

As a parent, it is important for you to recognize your child's ability to deal with abstract concepts, no matter what form of expression that ability takes. Whether he first uses language, gestures, spatial relationships or pretend play to express his ideas, you will want to encourage this development: Using ideas to manage feelings is an important milestone on the road to emotional maturity. It is a skill your child must master in order to bring the raw, self-centered impulses of his early childhood under control and to learn to live harmoniously with others.

The capacity to use ideas does not emerge full-blown overnight. It develops in stages that you can observe. In the first

The Parents' Role

Encourage your child to express ideas verbally.

● Talk to him even when he cannot understand. When he communicates with sounds and gestures, tell him what the real words would be.

● Teach him the names for his feelings: Does the music make you happy? Are you mad at me? Are you scared when the dog gets so close?

MOMMY!

The Parents' Role

Act as your youngster's partner in pretend play.

● Use any of the child's favorite activities — blocks, dress-up, puppets, dolls — as a framework for games that explore the feelings she displays in her normal behavior.

● To show her that all of her feelings are natural and acceptable, introduce a range of emotions into your games.

stage, which typically begins at about 18 months, the child will employ ideas simply to communicate something she wants. She may use words to ask for apple juice, gesture for her favorite blanket or tug at your leg for a hug.

To recognize the other stages of this learning process, it helps to focus on your child's pretend play. A second stage commences at about two years. In play, your child may have her teddy bear ask for a hug, then let a doll embrace the bear in response. In this simple exchange, the child moves beyond using ideas merely to state a demand. Now there is the idea of the teddy bear's demand plus the idea that the doll fulfills a role in responding to that need. At this stage, the child might say "Daddy, apple juice" rather than just blurting out "juice, juice."

At two and a half, the child's play is characterized by a random stream of ideas without concern for the kinds of constraints that adults take for granted. Logic, sequential time, cause and effect — all of these are missing. In the course of 10 minutes, the teddy bear might get in a fight, fall asleep on a lumpy bed of building blocks, fly on a plane one tenth his size and try to play a harmonica. Whatever occurs to the child is what happens next. Whatever props are nearby become part of the game. In this third level, the child is using a lot of ideas, but the ideas have little apparent connection.

In the fourth level, around the age of three, the child starts to fill in the first of those missing connections. Now the teddy bear may be seated in company at a rather elaborate tea party. The child's play begins to follow a somewhat more organized theme. Moment-to-moment details are still decided spontaneously, but there is an underlying plan and a unifying emotional thread that keeps the party on track. The child's feelings about taking care of her imaginary guests keep the game organized.

Sometime between three and four years old, the child reaches a fifth stage, making a dramatic leap in her ability to use ideas. She begins to experiment with her concepts about emotions and tries to mimic reality in pretend play. Now the bear might receive undivided attention throughout an elaborate reenactment of the child's own evening routine. There is dinner, a bath, then sympathy and help when the bear has trouble putting on his nightclothes. The game might continue with a bedtime story and tender words of love as the bear is tucked into bed. The child has begun to use pretend play as a testing ground for emotional expression, manipulating ideas in search of a cause-and-effect understanding. In essence, she is connecting emotional ideas in the same ways that grownups do. She has begun to think about feelings in an organized way.

The three-year-old serves tea to a group of toy friends in a reenactment of the many meals she has watched her mother prepare (inset). The little girl's pretend games have moved beyond simple imitation of random activities: The patterns of her tea parties now are more detailed and realistic, organized by her newfound social notions of how one should care for guests.

In Dr. Greenspan's view, the ability to connect and organize emotional ideas takes the youngster to a whole new plateau in her emotional learning. Trying out ways of organizing her own ideas and impressions about things around her, she begins to understand how the real world works. She is moving out of her self-centered cocoon — the young child's egocentric assumption that all things revolve around her and her needs — and into an awareness of a world of objects and feelings that are separate and different from herself. The child has made another major stride on her learning journey.

The most obvious way in which you will see your child testing her ideas is in her struggle to accept your standards for her behavior. Learning to follow rules really began when the child was about one and a half. When she first started to wander and explore, she was always looking back for reassurance. You could wag a finger or say "no" when she reached for the toilet or the stereo. Though she did not always do what she was told, her reactions showed that she had absorbed a sense of limits. Up to that point, however, limits meant following orders.

Now, at three or four, the child not only understands that certain actions are wrong, but she also experiences feelings of shame arising from her own misbehavior. Even if she only imagines a jealous assault upon a sibling, she may find herself suddenly stricken with pangs of guilt. As she learns the difference between "me" and "you," she sees that the limits once imposed by her parents are now coming from within. In pretend play, she may practice her newfound acceptance of limits by finding cause to discipline one of her dolls.

As your child gains experience socially and practices this new skill of self-imposed limits, he begins to appreciate shades and nuances of emotion. He discovers that sometimes he has to let the context be his guide in deciding how to express his feelings. Shouting angrily at a playmate is different from shouting at the teacher in nursery school. He also learns that every expression of emotion will produce an emotional reaction in response. If he tells you that the lasagna tastes terrible, your face may look exasperated or hurt. But if he screams out "Mama, I hate you," your face will very likely look either devastated or mad. When your child was just six months old he learned that his actions could produce a response. Now he sees that his ideas can have the same effect.

The child's first ideas about emotions were undistilled collections of everything she knew about a particular feeling. Her own experiences with feeling sad were mixed with everything that she could observe when she sensed that her mother was feeling

Scolded by her mother for some misdeed (inset), the child acts out a replay of the lesson by spanking her doll for an imagined transgression. Pretend play has become the girl's practice ground for emotional expression. At four years old, she is learning how the world works in terms of cause and effect: If she misbehaves, she is likely to be disciplined. In addition, the youngster may for the first time experience her own feelings of guilt.

45

The Parents' Role

Teach your child to be aware of other people and sensitive to their emotional needs.

● Empathize with your child's feelings, letting her know you understand. Meet her distress with comforting words and her joy with genuine enthusiasm.

From your example she will learn to empathize with others.

● Always try to respond to her questions and conversation. If she has to wait till you are free for you to give her your attention, tell her that, but do not ignore her or change the subject.

unhappy. It is only with time and experience that the child learns to distinguish between her own feelings and those of someone else. The same sense of "me" and "you" that helps the child accept limits enables her for the first time, at the age of three or four, to feel empathy or compassionate love. Now, when the child sees her mother sad, she may try to help with a special hug or a handful of flowers.

The preschooler's awareness of other people's feelings is part of a growing ability to categorize her experiences. Increasingly, she can perceive grown-up distinctions between self and other, animate and inanimate, right and wrong, real and make-believe, yesterday and today. Once she has grasped the distinction between yesterday and today — her first understanding of the concept of time — patience will follow, for she now can appreciate the promise of future rewards.

The result of all these developments is a set of skills that will be central to the child's social and emotional adjustment throughout the coming years. These are the skills that will enable her to focus her attention and follow rules in school, to distinguish between reality and fantasy in play, to plan a course of action and work toward a future goal in a job, and to consider the feelings and needs of those who share her life. Although her emotional abilities will continue to grow and change well into adulthood, the foundations are firmly laid by kindergarten age.

As Dr. Greenspan's studies reveal, two overriding tendencies propel your child through this course of emotional learning. One is his very basic need for a sense of order and control. It started at birth as a need to feel calm and continued as a search for ever more comprehensive ways to feel organized. The other is the child's eagerness to exercise each new emerging skill. During his early bonding phase, the baby seemed to hunger for your face. Later on, he was passionate about the lessons of pretend play. This second tendency — the child's enthusiasm for learning — is what allows you, the parent, to play a positive, ongoing role in his emotional growth.

As you observe your child's progress, remember that the path will not be entirely linear. There are bound to be some slips, some fits and starts. Particularly when your child is learning something new, he may regress in other areas that he has long since mastered. But these regressions will usually be short-lived and, overall, the pace of learning is remarkably rapid. By the age of five, your child will be standing on his own, emotionally equipped to march off to school and take his place in a world of other people. Like many accomplishments in life, the end of this journey is only a good beginning.

Touched by her mother's expression of unhappiness (inset), the five-year-old tries to help by presenting a handful of blossoms. Though such displays of empathy may be infrequent in early childhood, they should increase as the child matures: The ability to empathize with other people's feelings is a token of the full development of a youngster's emotional capacities.

Growing Pains

The life of an infant is enviably structured; everything is tailored to the child's personal needs. When she wants a warm bottle, a clean diaper or an undemanding play-mate, an attentive parent obliges. With the end of infancy, however, this comfortable pattern changes. No sooner does the child emerge from her parents' protective co-coon — tentatively walking, talking and asserting her independence — than the pressure to conform to the grown-up standards of family and society begins.

Suddenly the toddler is faced with a multitude of new ideas to comprehend and tasks to master. He is urged not to soil his diaper at all, but to recognize the purpose of the potty chair and anticipate his need to use it. Play no longer means grabbing a toy from another's hands to use or fling away at will; he must learn to share his toys and to consider the feelings of others. And parental praise, in the past so forthcoming, is now lavished or withheld on the basis of the child's actions.

The fast-paced lessons of early childhood, like any process of maturation and change, bring with them pre-dictable bouts of bewilderment and insecurity. A child's stressful feelings may take many odd forms: stub-born battles at bathtime or bedtime, thumb-sucking, toileting accidents after months of being trained. Al-though you may not immediately link such episodes to your youngster's development, these behaviors too are a normal — and often necessary — part of growing up.

Happily, they are also transitory, usually lasting only as long as it takes for your child to become comfortable at her new level of accomplishment.

Getting Along with Others

Over the course of your child's lifetime, his relationships with other people will be a major factor in his emotional well-being — as central to his happiness, probably, as good food and exercise are to his physical health. Yet babies do not come endowed at birth with the civilized spirit. It takes a few turbulent years, and usually more than a few tears, for the social skills to develop and mature.

The socializing process actually begins in infancy with the loving give-and-take between the parent and the child, a model for future social involvement that occurs long before a child shows any interest in playing with peers. But more specific training in getting along with others — sharing, taking turns, being friendly, generous and tactful — has to be keyed to a youngster's mental and emotional maturity. Before he can control his behavior on his own, a child must be able to remember what is expected of him and to understand how a certain behavior affects himself as well as others. These abilities advance at different rates in different children, much as physical growth varies, and parents will experience nothing but frustration and disappointment if they insist on trying to hurry their youngster along before he is ready.

From ego-centered to empathetic

As babies and toddlers, children envision themselves squarely at the center of the universe and understand their own needs only. This so-called egocentric viewpoint is not deliberately selfish, but simply a result of their inability at this stage to comprehend that other people have independent existences and feelings of their own. Watch a pair of two-year-olds playing in a sandbox: They seem hardly aware of each other's presence, until one decides suddenly she must have the pail and shovel her friend is holding, and snatches it away as though the other child were not there. The victim, surrendering the toys in wordless surprise, runs wailing to her mother for solace as her companion plays on unperturbed.

But then observe the same two friends after two years' passing. Chances are they will be working together on a sand castle, playing and chatting away so peaceably that their mothers feel no need for supervision at all. What has happened in the interim is a watershed development that experts have identified as the first stirrings of empathy: a widening of the child's self-absorbed viewpoint into a broader understanding of other people and their feelings. The growth of empathy between the third and fifth years, coupled with an increasing ability to detect and follow society's unwritten rules, will be the key to your child's social adjustment for the rest of her life.

The evolution of children's play

A child's pattern of play is a good guide to how far he has matured mentally and emotionally. At eighteen months, toddlers are already very interested in playing, but not with children their own age. Rather, their energies are directed toward exploring and mastering things — a toy car, a ball, a stacking tower of colorful rings.

Sometime during the third year, youngsters begin to enjoy the first stages of social play, playing side by side with another child, though with no real interaction, in what psychologists term "parallel play." Toddlers of this age, in the process of defining themselves as individual personalities, are absorbed in the lessons of "me," "my" and "mine." In their view, wanting something is tantamount to owning it, and sharing something seems the equivalent of losing it forever. These early play sessions are likely to be filled with frequent, though fleeting, conflicts.

By about four years of age, the well-adjusted child has broadened his play to include a greater degree of involvement with others. In this next stage, called "associative play," children still play separately and individually, but they begin to engage in social chatter. If you listen closely to the conversation between two children of this age, you will notice that they are not really talking to their playmate, but are conducting separate monologues, each child cheerfully talking about his own concerns without regard to the other's. "Me first" is still the ruling sentiment, and a certain amount of friction is inevitable: hitting and pushing and fighting over toys typically peak at this age.

Finally, by the age of five most youngsters add interludes of "cooperative play," working together at recreational tasks while engaging in conversations that show their newfound ability to listen and respond to each other. The years from three to five are an expansive period, a time when children actively seek out the company of their peers. Antisocial incidents are fewer now, becoming more verbal and less physical in nature as the children mature. Preschoolers, while aware that others have feelings, have not yet acquired the tact to handle them gently. Gathering in cliques and excluding unwanted playmates are unintentionally cruel ways that children of this age explore social bonds. Four-year-olds tend to be particularly bossy and boastful, although peer pressure will usually solve this problem by kindergarten age.

The role of social emotions

By the age of five or six, your child will have learned a great deal about social behavior, figuring out which actions please and displease by interpreting the verbal and facial expressions of the people around him. Through these trial-and-error lessons, he develops a whole new layer of complex emotional responses, the so-called social emotions that include embarrassment, envy, guilt, shame and pride.

As an infant, he used more basic emotional expressions — such inborn responses as distress, interest and fear — as wordless signals to communicate his fundamental needs to you *(pages 10 and 11)*. Like those primal emotions, these newer ones are survival tools, but their aim is social rather than physical survival. They signal to the child that his behavior is right or wrong according to the rules that govern the world he lives in, thus serving as signposts along the youngster's path to social acceptance.

He feels shame, for example, when he believes that someone he cares about has seen him do something that he knows is not allowed. Deep inside he may fear the loss of love and respect, and he will very likely — either consciously or subconsciously — adjust his behavior in the future to avoid that distressing possibility.

Guilt, by contrast, wells up in the socialized youngster when he senses privately that he has violated a rule and fears that punishment may result, or if the child realizes that he has failed to meet his own internalized standards of behavior. Because the process of absorbing other people's standards and making them truly your own takes time, guilt is usually the last social emotion to mature.

Both shame and guilt are negative emotions, sufficiently unpleasant that the socially mature child will eventually learn to avoid the antisocial behaviors that trigger them. The emotion of pride, on the other hand, comes when the child knows that he has measured up to the group's expectations. It rewards the child with good feelings, encouraging him to repeat the behavior that brought them on. Over time, these social emotions become powerful forces in molding the child's overall personality, in determining how well he succeeds in play, at school, in his family life.

How parents can help

While it is natural for young children to resist surrendering their infantile impulses to social regulation, youngsters who are basically well-adjusted and who feel loved will also be eager to please. Rest assured that with your patience and understanding, your child will eventually master the basic tenets of "do unto others," no matter how recalcitrant she may seem at the outset. From the time she begins the most rudimentary parallel play, you can start her on the road to winning friends by following a few simple guidelines.

Your first impulse may be to rush in and straighten things out when your child tangles with playmates, but you should resort to direct intervention only if you see that a situation is getting out of hand. However fierce these frays may seem to a grownup, to the little ones involved they are passing aggravations, quickly settled and soon forgotten. Whenever possible, give children a chance to work out their own problems; they will learn that a little friction and frustration in play is not really fatal, and they will get valuable practice in fending — and thinking — for themselves.

When you do feel the need to step into a dispute, to prevent someone from getting hurt or perhaps to bring a chaotic situation back under control, keep your messages short, direct and immediate. Lengthy sermons will go unheeded in the heat of the moment, and if you wait until things calm down to deliver the lesson, your advice will be difficult for the children to apply.

Even the youngest children may accept social rules more readily if they are shown the reasons. Rather than a flat "No!" try using "No: You line up on this end" to explain to a toddler why she must not butt into the front of a line. Older children can absorb a more detailed explanation: "Everyone wants to be first in line, but only one child can have that place, and she got there first." Pointing out what is gained by cooperative behavior — the fact that she will have more friends and fewer battles — lets the youngster know that your instructions are not merely parental whims.

The power of the positive

As in every other area of child rearing, you will get much more mileage from a pinch of positive reinforcement than from a bucketful of nagging criticism. Watch for opportunities to praise your youngster's positive behavior, and discourage antisocial actions not with scolding and punishment, but by demonstrating praiseworthy alternatives. If your toddler is overly possessive of his toys when other children visit, for example, you might ask him before a guest arrives to think about which toys he might like to share and which ones he wants to put away ahead of time. In this way, you reaffirm the importance of sharing while acknowledging the toddler's deep-seated need to own his toys. When sharing goes well, be sure to praise him — not just for being good, but specifically for sharing, which reinforces the concept once more in his mind and gives him a rush of pride that will prompt him to do it again.

It will probably take dozens of small lessons such as this one before your child is ready to practice the social graces on his own, but the ultimate goal — the abiding pleasures of having friends and being a friend to others — is well worth your efforts. •:•

An Urge for Independence

For your child, beginning to walk is more than the first step toward physical freedom. Moving about independently — opening a closet door, walking through a flower bed, pushing his stroller — he develops an entirely new view of himself as a separate person.

Yet this new awareness of self is frightening as well as exciting. Your child sits atop an emotional seesaw. At one end is his wish to be independent, to make his own choices and to break loose from your controls. At the other is his desire to remain the baby who can depend on you absolutely. One minute he insists that you leave him alone; the next, he wails for you to return. Over the next few years, the two of you will rock back and forth, trying to achieve a balance.

If you are unprepared for this inevitable experience, you may find it frustrating, even exasperating. The rebellious child of 18 months to three years old, with his stubbornness, unpredictable actions, rapid mood swings and negativism, can try the patience of even the saintliest parent. By the time he is three, much of the storm may have passed, and the transition from babyhood to childhood may seem largely accomplished. Your child's self-esteem and competence will have deepened, his emotional dependency on you lessened, and his view of the world widened to include other children. But the process is not truly complete. For years to come you will find that for short periods he suddenly becomes a baby again, cowed by the world, needing to cling to you for reassurance. A child's fashioning of his independent self continues through the preschool years and beyond.

"Me do it myself"

The struggle for independence begins with your toddler's insisting, "Me do it myself." She will demand to feed herself and put on her own coat. You should welcome these requests, since they show that she feels secure enough to attempt to manage things by herself.

Children learn by doing, so it is important that they try to do what their parents have been doing for them. Yet the projects they are determined to take on are often beyond their physical dexterity. A toddler will labor with mighty concentration to pour a glass of juice, and then dissolve into tears after spilling the whole carton on the floor. When you insist on pushing her in the stroller instead of letting her walk, she feels bullied. So many of her efforts at independence are frustrated — by you, by objects she cannot manage, by her own body.

Helping your child to succeed

Your child's emotional growth requires him to assert his independence from you, but he can accomplish this only with your help. The trick comes in encouraging his efforts while being attuned to what he can handle. When your two-year-old insists on zipping up his coat, you give him a head start by connecting the bottom of the zipper. He is successful because you have adapted the situation to his capabilities.

You can remove sources of frustration and help your child act independently by creating a physical environment that meets his needs. A small step-stool makes it possible for him to get to the sink to wash his hands. Dressing is made easier if you choose simple clothing, such as trousers with elastic waists. Each time that he successfully does something new, his self-confidence increases.

Let him make harmless mistakes. If he puts his T-shirt on backward, resist the temptation to correct it. By allowing the shirt to remain reversed, you avert a possible fight and, more importantly, provide him with a sense of accomplishment.

With all this insistence on independence, you may be surprised when your stubborn child suddenly changes his tune and insists, "You do it." Whether young children have managed a new challenge or met with failure, they often then want to retreat for a while until they feel more comfortable. Because the wish for dependency remains strong, even the four-year-old who has mastered dressing himself may occasionally ask you for help.

Setting limits

Your child also needs to learn what she may and may not do, and your reasons for any particular rules. When you forbid her to touch the stove, explain why. Remember that some rules will change as your child matures, and you will need to reevaluate them continually. Setting limits for your child is critical to fostering her autonomy. She can maintain her sense of security — the foundation stone of independence — only when she feels sure of her boundaries.

How you set limits affects your child's personal growth. If you boss her around, telling her to "Do it because I say so," you stifle her efforts to use her own initiative and leave her dependent, unhappy and angry. If instead you exercise little or no authority, letting her do practically anything she pleases, even things that hurt or disturb other people, you again deprive her of real independence. Without any clear boundaries, she is groping in the dark, feeling unsure of herself. You promote competence and autonomy in your child by being rational, firm, and consistent, yet warm and loving.

The almighty "no"

Saying "no," just like saying "me" and "mine," is a powerful way for children to assert their separateness. By disagreeing with whatever you are proposing, your child brings you up short and forces you to treat her as an individual. Some toddlers say no so relentlessly that they even say it when what they really mean is yes.

All young children go through such periods of negativism. They will ignore direct questions, do the opposite of what they are told and dawdle when they sense that Mother is in a particular hurry. At the same time that they are bolstering their autonomy with this behavior, they are also testing the rules to de-

termine what is expected of them and learning how to create boundaries for themselves. Negativism usually peaks around the third birthday. Its intensity and form of expression varies from child to child. Your child is most likely to rebel at mealtime, bathtime or bedtime, or whenever you issue a command.

Handling negativism Try to manage your dealings with your child to reduce the opportunities for personal clashes. When you must assert your will, try suggesting, "Let's do something else," rather than flatly declaring, "No, don't do that." Avoid asking questions such as "Do you want to take your bath now?" that automatically elicit a negative response.

Try using games to accomplish a task or to get through a touchy situation. When you want your child to pick up toys, offer a challenge: "Let's see how fast we can get these toys back into the box." Knowing the potential problem areas — cleaning up, taking a nap or eating lunch — you can steer your youngster around them without his sensing your guidance.

Decision making Making her own decisions is another way in which your child asserts her independence. Sometimes she finds it easy to do, and once she makes up her mind, she stands firm. She wants to wear her mittens on a warm summer day, despite all your arguments as to why she should not. By all means, let her. Unless she has freedom to make wrong decisions — short of those that are dangerous or that are obnoxious to others — she will never learn how to make decisions at all.

At other times you will observe that decision making, particularly for the toddler, becomes upsetting, even painful, because many of her own feelings are still a mystery to her. Perhaps you give her the choice of going to the post office with you or staying at home with the other parent. As soon as you offer these alternatives, your child becomes confused and tense. With her short memory and few similar experiences to draw upon, she does not know which choice she would enjoy more, and having to decide torments her. Children are much more comfortable with questions such as "Which candy do you want to eat first?" since they know that they will soon get to eat both.

Temper tantrums When your child has to struggle to master a task or makes a demand that you refuse to meet, he feels frustrated by his helplessness. Sometimes his frustration and anger well up suddenly and uncontrollably, and he erupts in a spontaneous display of emotion that alarms him as much as it does you. In the classic temper tantrum, familiar to generation after generation of parents but nonetheless disturbing to any grownup who is confronted with one, the child screams, kicks and flails wildly about. He may fling toys or other objects. Some children hold their breath until they turn blue in the face, in an effort to frighten their parents. Usually within a few minutes, the outburst ends and the child's sunny disposition returns.

Temper tantrums occur most frequently between the ages of one and three. More than half of all two-year-olds have tantrums once or twice a week. If your toddler is active, energetic and determined, he may be particularly prone to tantrums. The ignition points for each child are different, but most children will explode into a tantrum when frustrated, hungry, overtired or overexcited. Tantrum behavior decreases as children mature psychologically and are able to express their protests verbally.

Weathering tantrums When a tantrum erupts, stay calm. It is frightening for a child to lose control of herself and even scarier if a grownup follows suit. Do not try to reason with her, and do not argue, scream back or threaten punishment. If your child is given to mild tantrum behavior, your best bet is to ignore it by turning your back, possibly even leaving the room. You are telling her that this outburst has no effect on you. Under no circumstances should you reward your child for this behavior — by offering candy in hopes of diverting her, for instance — or reveal that the tantrum upsets you. If you do, you are likely to see more, not less, of it.

However, if a tantrum is so severe that you think your child might actually injure herself or another child, you should gently but firmly pick her up and move her away from the scene. It is best to stay with her, either holding her in your arms or simply remaining close by, until the emotions have subsided. With violent tantrums, many experts feel, a child's need for support and comfort outweighs any concerns the parent might have about encouraging such behavior.

Few moments are so embarrassing for parents as when their children throw tantrums on the playground or in a department store, but you should not let the oh-you-cruel-mother stares from passersby induce you into special handling. Your child needs your firmness and control now more than ever. If possible, pick her up and move her away from the source of stimulation. If not, stand your ground by holding her firmly until the outburst is over.

After a while you will learn to watch for storm signals and head off the tempest. Organize your child's life so that her frustration level stays within the limits of her tolerance. For example, do not take your child on a shopping expedition when she really needs a nap.

Beyond the aggravation Although your child's assertiveness, negativism and temper tantrums may sometimes leave you weary, remember that they are a necessary part of growth, signs of budding independence that show that your child is in the process of defining her own special self. ❖

Retreating from the whirl of her frenetic day, she finds comfort in her familiar blanket and thumb.

The Terrific "Terrible Twos"

No other phase of childhood is so misunderstood, misnamed or mistakenly maligned as the notorious "terrible twos." To begin with, the behavior patterns that distinguish this period are not restricted to two-year-olds, being found in children from the age of 18 months or even younger, right up into the preschool years. And — as is evidenced by this photographic diary of a two-year-old named Sarah — the behavior of a child at this stage of development hardly deserves to be termed terrible, however irrepressible, unpredictable and, at times, even unlikable it may be.

In fact, for parents who understand what lies behind their child's erratic actions, the so-called "terrible twos" may be viewed as a kind of birth — the birth of an independent social being. The child enters this stage a baby, so totally dependent for every physical and psychological need that she is practically an extension of her parents. Within a year or so, she emerges as a separate person, capable of making decisions, asserting her will and, relatively speaking, taking care of herself.

To guide a youngster through this remarkable transformation is a moving and memorable experience, if often an exhausting one. As these pictures indicate, a child of two or thereabouts sets a dizzyingly fast pace of instantly changing moods, intermingling enthusiastic bursts of activity with quiet withdrawal, sweet compliance with stubborn negativism, joyful interest with tired or angry tears.

By watching closely to learn what causes such emotional swings in your child, you can take steps to ease the struggle for independence, help build her confidence and ensure that the happy times predominate. In addition to insight, you will need a healthy portion of patience, a firm will and, if Sarah is typical, a great deal of stamina and a comforting pair of arms.

Undaunted by her precarious perch, Sarah boldly explores a cupboard for forbidden marshmallows.

The child nestles tearfully in her mother's arms, her independence temporarily dissolved by a bump suffered in adventurous play.

By sweeping up a bowl she has broken, Sarah learns a new skill as well as a lesson in responsibility.

"Do it myself" is the two-year-old's typical impulse in dress and grooming, though frustrations abound.

A determined Sarah measures out water for a game, heeding her mother's warning not to make a mess.

Stress-Related Habits

Children feel stress, even in their earliest months, when they are bothered by such things as hunger, boredom or fatigue. Toddlers worry about mastering new skills, including talking, using the toilet and socializing. There are rules to learn, and ever-increasing pressures to act in more acceptable, less baby-like ways. In addition, children may be confronted with sudden, worrisome changes such as a transfer to another day-care center, a move to a new home, or the appearance of a new brother or sister.

Children need to relieve the tensions these experiences cause, but they lack the ability to talk them out or think them through. Physical activity helps, and play is an important therapy for stress. But sometimes a youngster will seek additional comfort in an activity such as thumb-sucking, clinging to a favorite toy, or rocking back and forth.

This kind of behavior usually soon outlives its usefulness as a tension-reliever and is abandoned before it becomes a problem. If you view the activity as a bad habit that must be stopped, or worry that it is evidence of abnormality, you may add to the stress that prompted the behavior in the first place. Your best reaction is patience; the less attention you call to the activity, the more likely the child is to drop it at an early age. You should be concerned, and seek the advice of a doctor, only if the habit is greatly prolonged or exaggerated, or is accompanied by withdrawal from play and friends. If you notice your child engaging in several tension-relieving habits simultaneously, this may also indicate a need for professional attention.

Thumb-sucking
Your baby is born with a normal and necessary desire to suck, the intensity of which varies from child to child. At any time after birth, your baby may begin to suck her thumb or finger, even her lip or tongue, to satisfy that urge. Breast-fed babies are less likely to become thumb-suckers, because mothers generally allow them to linger longer at the breast than bottle-fed babies at a bottle.

When a baby is weaned, the need to suck for food declines, but sucking — usually of a thumb or a pacifier — continues to be a comforting and calming activity for the child. It is not a sign of significant insecurity, but your youngster is most likely to suck when she feels tired, upset or bored, or when she is or trying to fall asleep. You need not be concerned, even if she irritates her thumb or displaces her baby teeth slightly. Neither effect is long-lasting. Most likely, she will drop the habit by kindergarten age. Trying to talk her out of it before she is ready may only increase her determination. Arm restraints, bitter coatings and adhesive strips are not effective.

If thumb-sucking persists beyond the age of six, however, the child risks displacing the upper permanent teeth, and she should be discouraged from continuing the practice. The way to do this is indirectly, by dealing with the causes of the behavior rather than by forbidding it. For example, if the youngster sucks when she is tired, try an earlier bedtime. Counter boredom with parental attention or stimulating play, hunger with a snack and so on.

The Thumb-Sucking Problem

66 With five kids, I'm not about to get excited because the middle one, Kevin, sucks his fingers. It's interesting, though, he sucks the third and fourth fingers of his left hand — palm up! I can't figure out how he got comfortable with that awkward position. When he was still sucking his fingers raw at the age of four, I got worried about infection. My mother reminded me that some babies need to suck and be cuddled more than others. I started holding Kevin on my lap while I read him a bedtime story. Sometimes, by the end of the story, the fingers creep into his mouth, but by then he's so sleepy I slide them out as I put him into bed. Outside of lots of hugs and attention, that's about all I can do. Or want to do. 99

66 My daughter sucked her thumb so long that the top half of it started to flatten out. I was a little worried about her teeth, but decided not to be too concerned until her permanent teeth came in. When she started school, she would cover her face with a handkerchief during naptime so no one would see her thumb in her mouth. About this time she started to tell me she was too old to be sucking her thumb. Peer pressure was getting to her. She tried to stop, but found it hardest at night, and eventually decided on her own that the only way she could do it was to wear gloves to bed. I could have cried when I saw her in her pajamas and her little white cotton gloves, but they did the trick. 99

66 As Lisa's thumb-sucking continued into her second year, I wondered if I had taken her off the bottle too early, but my pediatrician reassured me that some children seem to need to suck more than others. Lisa turned two, then three and four, and still she sucked her thumb and clutched her favorite blanket when she was tired or bored, or when her older sisters and playmates got to be too much for her. The blanket shrank and became tattered, and the satin binding hung in shreds. Then, when she was five, things changed. After a few days in kindergarten, obviously stung by the teasing of her classmates, Lisa insisted, 'I am not a baby!' She began to take her thumb out of her mouth and dry it on the doll-size blanket. Before long she stopped sucking altogether. 99

66 I stopped four of my five children from sucking their thumbs simply by pulling their hands away from their mouths. I know a lot of doctors don't approve of that method, but I thought it was better than coating their thumbs with pepper sauce, which is what my sister-in-law did to her kids. But my daughter Bonnie was so determined to suck that I bought her a pacifier. Her father was unhappy about that, he thought pacifiers were unsanitary. One day he lost his temper about it, grabbed the pacifier, took it outside and threw it over the fence into a vacant lot. 'That's the end of that,' he said. But it wasn't, not quite yet. Late that night, while Bonnie howled ceaselessly for her pacifier, he was out in the weeds with a flashlight searching for it. He couldn't find it. She eventually went to sleep, and she never sucked a pacifier or her thumb again. 99

Comfort objects

At about six months of age, your baby begins to sense for the first time that he is separate from you. He craves more independence, yet at the same time the child feels acutely anxious about losing his closeness to you. He may respond to this conflict by striking a compromise and clinging to a substitute parent in the form of a teddy bear, blanket or pacifier. This object is something the child can control, and it offers comfort and familiarity.

It does no harm for a child whose social skills are developing well to become entranced with a comfort object. He may talk with it, invest it with special powers, weave rituals around it, even become attached to its grubbiness or smell. Do not try to take his object away from him. The youngster will most likely outgrow his need for it between the ages of two and five.

However, there are some things you can do to limit the habit and make it easier for you to live with it. In the early stages you can restrict use of the comfort object to home or bedtime. When the object gets dirty, wash it while the child is asleep. If it is a blanket, cut a piece of it off to save as a backup in case he loses the prized object — unless you think you and your child can survive "cold-turkey" withdrawal.

Remind him occasionally that when he is a big boy he will no longer need his special comforter. Of course, you should not accept any and all uses of a comfort object. For example, do not let your child keep a feeding bottle in his bed and fall asleep sucking it; not only emotional attachment, but tooth decay as well, could result.

Rocking   When your child is about nine months old, he may begin rhythmic movements — rolling his head, rocking on his hands and knees, even banging his head on the end of the crib. Rocking usually occurs when the youngster is tired and trying to fall asleep. The habit, which may be an attempt to recreate the comfort of being rocked by you, will probably wane when the child begins to crawl, although it may persist as long as the age of four.

The best thing to do is to let the behavior run its course, unless the rocking becomes prolonged or extends into the child's normal waking hours. You may want to cut down on the noise by padding the crib, and putting it on a thick rug or anchoring its legs. You should consult a doctor if head-banging begins, however, since this activity may become vigorous enough to cause bruises.

There are ways you can help prevent rocking from becoming exaggerated. During the day, spend as much time as possible with your child and cuddle him often. Keep the youngster occupied, and encourage him to vent his feelings at play. Prolong the child's bedtime rituals in order to reduce tension; a warm bath may help, and so may rhythmic music. Try not to leave your child alone in the crib until you see that he is ready to fall asleep.

Hair-pulling   Children often play idly with their hair, twirling strands of it in their fingers or even tugging it, and all these activities are quite normal. But yanking on the hair continually and vigorously, perhaps even tearing out patches of it, is not. It may be a sign that the child is experiencing significant stress, and a reason for consulting a doctor to try to find the underlying problem.

While there is no direct remedy for the habit, there also appear to be no long-term ill effects. Note the circumstances that tend to set off your child's hair-pulling, then try to avert them or at least distract the child from them. Consider cutting the hair to make it less inviting to grasp. Or try providing a substitute whose hair can be pulled instead, such as a long-haired doll or a furry stuffed toy.

Nail-biting   Casual biting of the nails is a common activity among children, usually after they reach the age of three or four. An otherwise happy child, finding herself bored, a little worried or excited, perhaps by a television program, may bite her fingernails. Nagging about the practice never helps, but instead focuses attention on, and probably prolongs, an activity that otherwise might quickly pass.

Nail-biting that continues for an extended period is usually seen only in children five or older, and often as a response to a specific worry. Try to identify what may be specially troubling your child, and help her deal with it. Think of new activities that involve use of the hands. Encourage pride in the appearance of the hands by emphasizing good grooming, even allowing her to use clear nail polish.

If the nail-biting persists and becomes compulsive — if your child gnaws constantly at her nails and keeps them bitten to the quick — you should get medical advice.

Bed-wetting Many children wet their beds occasionally until they are four or five years old, and it is not uncommon for these accidents to persist to the age of seven. But if they do not decrease in frequency after the age of four, or if they appear after the child has been dry for some time, there is evidently a problem, and you should consult your doctor. As inconvenient and distressing as these accidents may be to your child and you, they are in all probability the result of some minor and temporary cause, such as a bladder that has not grown quite fast enough, an inherited trait or some unavoidable stress.

The most important thing is to remain calm and confident, treating the problem for what it is: a temporary delay in your child's gaining full control over urination. Your youngster will be anxious about his bed-wetting, and disappointed with himself every time it happens. Critical comments or punishment will only help to set up a discouraging cycle of worry and failure.

Assure the child (and yourself) that he will soon gain the control over urination that he needs and wants. Minimize the fuss over the bed-wetting accidents when they happen, and offer praise and rewards to your youngster when they do not. Just remember to keep your tone light, and not to equate dryness with goodness; that just makes the self-recrimination worse if another accident occurs.

Stuttering Until your child is about six years old, she may occasionally stutter. This repetition of sounds, syllables, words or even phrases is a normal stage of speech development. Stresses such as intensified toilet training or increased discipline may bring on a bout of stuttering, which in most cases will gradually disappear in a month or two if you react calmly and do not try to attack the stuttering problem directly.

Instead, play games with your child that require less talking and more physical activity. Let her take the lead more often, and be sure to give her your full attention when she talks, letting her know that you enjoy conversation with her. Do not expect an immediate change, but the problem should gradually disappear in a few months. If it does not, you should seek special training and medical advice. ❖

The Tribulations
of Toilet Training

The beginning of toilet training is a bewildering time for your child. He has no idea what you have in mind when you first place him on a potty chair and indicate that you want him to do something. When the youngster does somehow produce, it makes even less sense that you express great interest and delight in his achievement — and then consign it to the large white machine in the bathroom that roars and gurgles and sweeps things away.

However you choose to handle the practical aspects of toilet training, you should be aware of the emotional impact the process is likely to have on your toddler. You can expect him to feel some hesitation and anxiety, which may be expressed as all-out rebellion. He cannot know that your real aim in this adventure is to help him achieve his first measure of control over his own body, which will lift him to a new level of proud self-sufficiency. Nor does he realize that his success in toileting will shape his eventual attitudes toward cleanliness, responsibility and orderly ways of doing things for the rest of his life. For the moment, all the child knows is that his otherwise reasonable mother is behaving very peculiarly.

The importance of timing

The whole business is even more mystifying if you start the process too soon. The nervous system of a child under 18 months of age is not yet developed enough to give her control over the muscles that regulate bowel movements, and bladder control comes even later. What is more, a child that young cannot be expected to understand what you want her to do.

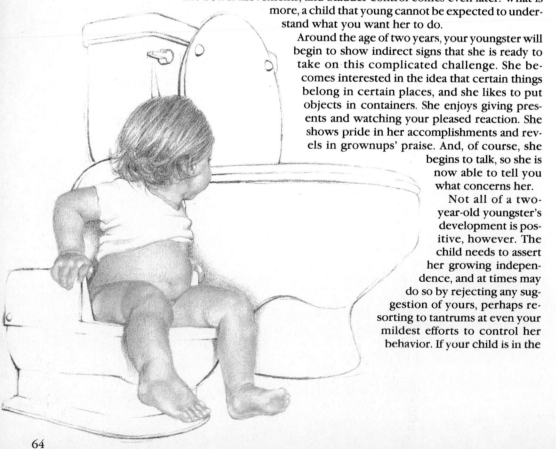

Around the age of two years, your youngster will begin to show indirect signs that she is ready to take on this complicated challenge. She becomes interested in the idea that certain things belong in certain places, and she likes to put objects in containers. She enjoys giving presents and watching your pleased reaction. She shows pride in her accomplishments and revels in grownups' praise. And, of course, she begins to talk, so she is now able to tell you what concerns her.

Not all of a two-year-old youngster's development is positive, however. The child needs to assert her growing independence, and at times may do so by rejecting any suggestion of yours, perhaps resorting to tantrums at even your mildest efforts to control her behavior. If your child is in the grip of such a phase, it is best to delay toilet training for a while. Keep her in diapers and try again in a few months. Whenever you do begin the training effort, select a time that is as free of other stresses as possible — not, for example, just after moving to a new house or bringing home a baby brother or sister.

Setting a relaxed tone You will be doing both yourself and your little one a favor during this period if you keep your own emotions in check and approach the task calmly, with an air of helpful, relaxed guidance. Your role is to suggest, remind, encourage and praise. Coercion, nagging or anger will only make the job more difficult. When your child has an accident, treat it casually and clean up without comment, other than to suggest in a reassuring way that "Maybe next time you'll be able to use the potty instead." Keep any feelings of disgust to yourself; your young trainee may be more ashamed of his failures than you can imagine, and he needs your support and comfort, not your disapproval.

Despite your understandable interest in the toilet-training process, it is best not to be too attentive or demonstrative. Overreacting, whether with pleasure or anger, shows the child that his actions control your feelings — a situation that may make him feel anxious or insecure. Resist the impulse to discuss his progress with relatives or friends in his presence. After all, you are not judging him in a contest, but encouraging him in a learning process.

Predictable behavior Although some children achieve the goal in a month or so, it is far more likely to take several months, and to be marked by odd behavior and frustrating setbacks. Do not be surprised, for instance, if your child develops a keen interest in what she has deposited in her potty. Letting her satisfy her quite natural curiosity with a close inspection, perhaps even a touch, usually takes care of the matter.

If your child resists using the toilet or has many accidents, do not mistake it for deliberate contrariness on her part. A fear of the big, noisy toilet underlies much toileting anxiety. Some toddlers withhold bowel movements to the point of becoming constipated, with resulting discomfort that causes even more anxiety. You may also witness unusual displays of fussiness or defiance during bathtime, mealtime or dressing. Children often act this way when they are feeling angry over the pressure to use the toilet, or when they secretly fear that they cannot measure up to their parents' expectations.

Anything that temporarily creates tension can result in backsliding in training: a family illness, a big trip, a new baby-sitting arrangement. Whatever the causes of such setbacks, never belittle or shame a child for having accidents: This can only lead to further anxiety and greater loss of control. With patience and persistence, you will see your youngster through these minor difficulties and soon leave the diaper era behind for good. What is more, you will have strengthened the trust between the two of you and increased your child's confidence in facing other challenges in the years to come. •:•

Sleep Problems

"When is he *ever* going to sleep through the night?" you may mutter resentfully as your child's cry awakens you in the pitch-dark hours after midnight. It is only natural for you to feel exhausted, exasperated, worried and perhaps even angry, especially if your baby or toddler has already interrupted your sleep one or more times since you fell into bed after a wearying day. The night shift can be the most trying part of parenting, especially when your child has sleep problems.

That is one reason — for the sake of your own physical and emotional health — to make a conscious effort to instill good sleep habits from the start. Another very important motive is, of course, your youngster's well-being. A child whose bedroom becomes a battleground for nightly struggles with parents over the issue of going to bed, going to sleep, or going back to sleep after awakening at night is unlikely to be among the happiest of children, or the most well-rested. The excessive conflict he is experiencing each night may spill over into his daytime behavior, especially if he teeters on the edge of fatigue during much of the day.

How much sleep is necessary?

Before you can help your child develop successful sleeping routines, you need some idea of how much sleep she actually needs (*chart, below*). Having a realistic understanding of what to expect helps keep down your level of frustration. While a newborn will sleep about 16½ hours out of every 24, the average six-month-old baby will need only slightly more than 14 hours. After that, the number of hours the average child sleeps drops about an hour each year until the age of four. Pre-schoolers average about 11 to 11½ hours of sleep a night.

The timing and length of sleep periods also change as children grow older. A newborn may spread her sleep over six or seven periods evenly distributed throughout the day and night. But by six months, she probably will be napping only twice during the daytime and, if you have helped her form good sleep habits, will have settled into regular overnight sleep, waking you only occasionally. Your child will most likely abandon her morning nap early in her second year, while her afternoon naps may continue until three years of age or even later.

Although such information can serve as a yardstick for roughly assessing your child's sleep patterns, do not worry yourself by making close

As this chart indicates, a child's need for sleep decreases markedly between birth and six years of age, in both the total time spent sleeping and the number of sleep periods in a 24-hour cycle. Bear in mind that these figures are averages and that the needs of individual children vary.

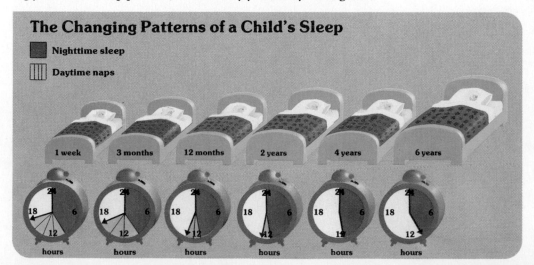

The Changing Patterns of a Child's Sleep

■ Nighttime sleep

▥ Daytime naps

1 week	3 months	12 months	2 years	4 years	6 years
hours	hours	hours	hours	hours	hours

comparisons. The figures are averages, and each child is an individual. For example, some perfectly normal, healthy two-and-a-half-year-olds may need only nine hours of sleep at night, especially if they nap well during the day. Others, equally fit, may snooze for 13 hours at night and may even get another one to two hours during the day. But if your child's total daily sleeping time differs by several hours from what is indicated for her age group on the chart, and if she consistently seems tired, irritable or overactive during the day, you should consider the possibility that she has a sleeping problem and take steps to eliminate it.

Different forms of sleep

To understand a child's sleep problem, you need to know something about the nature of a child's sleep. A full-term infant emerges from the womb already practiced in two distinct modes of sleeping known as active sleep and quiet sleep. The form called active sleep in newborn infants is also known as rapid eye movement (REM) sleep. It is distinguished by slight but frequent body movements, irregular breathing, changes in facial expression and the easily visible rapid movement of the baby's eyes beneath his closed eyelids. In older children, dreaming takes place during REM sleep *(page 84)*.

In the quiet sleep mode, the infant's breathing is regular and deep, and most other body movement is markedly diminished. In the first month, however, you may see fast body twitches, called startles, and rhythmical sucking motions while the baby is sleeping in this state.

At birth, a full-term baby divides his sleeping time roughly in half between active and quiet sleep. Until the age of three months, the baby falls directly into active, REM sleep; after about three months, he falls first into non-REM, or quiet sleep. During the first six months of life, the quiet mode of sleep evolves into varying stages similar to that seen in older children and in adults. When the child is in the deeper stages of non-REM sleep, he can be very difficult to awaken. It is this kind of sleep that enables you to dress him in his pajamas and tuck him into bed without waking him up when he falls asleep on the sofa or floor.

By the time he is six months old, his sleep moves through cycles of non-REM and REM sleep in a way which will remain fairly constant throughout life. While in REM sleep he may awaken, if only for a few seconds. He may open his eyes, examine his surroundings and shift his position. He might do this as often as nine or 10 times a night. You yourself, in fact, awaken the same way many times a night and usually return to sleep so promptly that later you do not remember being awake. If your baby learns to be a good sleeper, he, too, will fall quickly back into slumber from his nocturnal awakenings.

An infant's need for reassurance

It is not wise, however, to try to achieve this ideal state by ignoring the nighttime cries of your very young infant. In the first few months of your baby's life, you should be more concerned with responding to her needs than worried about establishing a correct sleep pattern. If she is crying at night, it is probably because she is wet or cold or hungry or uncomfortable, and you can solve those problems for her. The quicker

A Cozy Routine for Bedtime

A toddler finds security in a bedtime routine made up of almost-ceremonial steps. Here the ritual includes a bedtime story and Mommy kissing Teddy good night. It is important to leave the room while the child is still awake (far right), so she will learn to go to sleep on her own.

you answer her call for help, the easier she will be to soothe. If good sleep patterns do not develop on their own, you can take remedial steps later.

How to put your baby to bed

What you can do, during these early months, is establish a bedtime routine that will help your baby build good sleeping habits. It is perfectly natural for a mother or father to want to rock a new baby to sleep every night. That is, after all, one of the supreme pleasures of being a parent. But by the age of three months, many babies are ready to start sleeping through the night. That is, they no longer need a middle-of-the-night feeding and are far enough along in their sleep development that they pass the night moving through various stages of sleep broken intermittently by brief arousals. If your baby has learned that the only way to fall asleep is to be rocked, he will not know how to get back to sleep when he awakens alone in his crib. He may not be cold or hungry, and his diaper may even be dry. He is tired and ready to return to sleep. But where are the cuddling arms? Where is the rocking motion? He has no choice but to summon your assistance in the only way he knows: He takes a lungful of air and starts howling.

Unless you enjoy rocking your baby so much that you want to do it several times a night, you may wish, by the time your child is five or six months old, to alter the way you put him to bed in the first place. You need not deny yourself the joy of rocking him, but rock him when he is wakeful. That way your baby gets a bonus: He is fully aware of the pleasure of snuggling in your arms. When it is bedtime, put him into his crib in his favorite sleeping position, tuck him in, kiss him good night and turn off the lights, perhaps leaving a night light on.

Leave the room so he will get used to falling asleep alone. If he protests, you can pick him up and cuddle him, or do some quiet chore such as sorting his laundry. Or you can leave the door ajar and give evidence of your presence just outside his room by talking and making other soft noises as you move about. In most cases, a few evenings of this routine is sufficient for your baby to learn how to go to sleep on his own, and he will apply that experience whenever he awakens in the middle of the night. But if your child reaches the age of five or six months and is still demanding your attention throughout the night, you may wish to try the special sleep training program that appears on page 71, devised by a pediatrician specializing in sleep problems.

Should your child sleep with you?

Some parents swear that the best way for everybody to get a good night's sleep is for everybody, parents and baby, to sleep in the same bed or the same room. Their reasoning is that the baby soon gets onto the same sleep cycle as the parents and thus never awakens them during the night. They also contend that the child develops a feeling of security that he simply cannot achieve when he sleeps by himself. Some authorities maintain, however, that this arrangement actually makes it harder

for anyone to get a good night's sleep. And they say that many parents who use it only do so because it is easier than compelling a child to get back in his own bed when he arrives in his parents' room at four or so in the morning. Where you want your child to sleep is a purely personal matter, of course. But if you are considering this arrangement, you should bear in mind that once your child starts sleeping with you, it may be extremely difficult to switch back to separate accommodations, because the child will be so unhappy about being displaced.

Maintaining good sleep habits

Even if your baby takes readily to drifting off to sleep on her own, your troubles may not be over. At some point between seven and nine months, she may suddenly begin to protest with anguished cries your departure from her room each night. Her panic is a sign of separation anxiety, which emerges at about this time in a child's life. She has become strongly attached to you and does not yet understand that when someone disappears from view, that person continues to exist and will return. She is afraid you are going away forever.

Soon after this time, the baby's drive to master body skills such as walking becomes so intense that she often finds it difficult to unwind for sleep. You may discover her in the middle of the night crawling around in her crib or pulling herself up to a standing position, as though her drive to practice her skills outweighed her need for sleep.

Help your baby find her own methods for soothing herself to sleep, while reassuring her that you are not abandoning her. One way to accomplish this double purpose is to casually leave and reenter the room several times after she has been put to bed, making reassuring sounds but concerning yourself with some other bit of business rather than hovering over your protesting child. Parents sometimes interfere too much at bedtime, when their babies really just need a chance to complain a little before settling down to some humming or jabbering and then to sleep. Small gestures can help ease a baby's resistance to sleep. Let your child have a favorite toy or blanket for comfort when you leave the room. A night light that allows her to see her familiar surroundings when she awakens at night might also help.

Putting a toddler to bed

When your child is two or two and a half, you may find yourself a participant in a series of bedtime rituals that are a toddler's way of making the transition from being awake with plenty of company to being asleep alone. All the simple, practical processes are elaborated into a carefully choreographed ceremony: the bath, brushing the teeth, putting on pajamas, and selecting the right stuffed animal and the right book for the bedtime story. Everything must be in the same sequence every night or the spell is broken, so beware of adding any new elements that disrupt the ritual. Also beware of the delaying tactics that some children try to slip into the ceremonial routine: I want to change pajamas; I want another drink of water; I left something downstairs.

Your child may be more skittish about sleep on days when he has endured long separations from you or when he has experienced other daytime worries. The proverbial monster waiting at the foot of the bed often rears its head during this period of childhood. You should demonstrate to your child that you are in charge and able to protect him — even if it requires your loudly banishing the demon from the house.

Try to make bedtime the same time every night or as nearly the same time as possible. But keep your attitude toward your child's sleep positive and nonpunitive. If he is having trouble getting to sleep, do not try to force or threaten him. Your child needs to be shown, instead, that sleep is a welcome and pleasurable retreat. You can help foster this attitude by teaching him to cherish his bedroom as a pleasant haven for comfort, rest and security, rather than making it seem like a place that he is banished to for punishment.

Although many children consistently go to bed voluntarily, some do not, especially when the rest of the family is awake and doing interesting things. Give a 10-minute and a five-minute warning as the time to start the bedtime ritual nears. If your child insists on putting up a fight about going to bed, try a neutral signaling device, such as an alarm clock. This way, the source of the unwelcome news is impersonal, and the child cannot argue with it. Let him know that you understand how much he does not want to go to bed, but tell him firmly that it is, nonetheless, his bedtime. If he is playing, assure him that in the morning, he can return to what he was doing. Sometimes children feel less victimized when they are given options: "You can either go get in bed now, or you can kiss me good night and then get in bed."

Night wanderers Once they learn how to climb out of their cribs, some toddlers not only wake up in the middle of the night — they get up. This is when you may have to decide whether you are going to let your child get in bed with you or be firm about her returning to her own bed. Other children, especially those three years or older, actually get out of bed and walk about without waking up. The sleepwalking child's eyes will be wide open, but when you try to talk to her you will realize that she does not know what is happening. Sleepwalking episodes can be as brief as a few seconds or as long as half an hour. Try to get her back into bed without awakening her. Later, she will not recall the incident. Children usually grow out of a sleepwalking problem, but persistent, frequent episodes may indicate some underlying disturbance that should be explored with your pediatrician, a child psychologist or a sleep clinic. ❖

Training Your Child to Go to Sleep

Sleep problems caused by actual medical disorders are rare. If your child is six months old or older and still has to be rocked in order to get to sleep, or regularly wakes you up by crying in the middle of the night, the problem can almost always be attributed to habit. His habit, in effect, is you. He depends on your presence as a requirement for getting to sleep, in the same way that you might depend on, say, a pillow. When he awakens during the night, he needs you there to get back to sleep. And, just as you could train yourself to sleep without a pillow, you can teach your child to go to sleep without your help.

Some parents try to do this "cold turkey," letting their child cry until he falls asleep from exhaustion. But I believe this method is too harsh. The child may be confused by the abrupt change from his parents' normal response to his cries. He may become angry and distressed when they do not come running as usual. It is also painful for his parents to ignore his pleas. In fact, this method often fails because the parents give in. And if they finally pick up the child and comfort him and let him fall asleep in their arms, his tears will have been wasted.

I believe a gradual approach is better. The parent leaves the child alone, then returns to the child's room for a brief period, then leaves again. The parent repeats this pattern, gradually lengthening the time that the child is left on his own, until the child stops crying and falls asleep. Parents who have come to our pediatric sleep-clinic seeking help have had great success with this system, following the timetable presented below.

The technique is easy to apply, but it does require pa-

tience, consistency and stamina. Use a clock or watch in order to be precise about the times involved. On the first evening, put your child to bed after a bedtime story or other routine appropriate for his age, then leave the room. As the chart indicates, if your child begins to cry and is still crying at the end of five minutes, return to the room. Your purpose is simply to let him know that you are still caring for him, that he has not been abandoned. Stay only a minute or two. Do not pick him up, but you may offer a few words of reassurance. Then leave again, and this time stay away for 10 minutes. If he is still crying, go back to his room for another brief visit. After that, wait 15 minutes before returning a third time. For the rest of the first night, wait 15 minutes between visits. Of course, if he stops crying, do not enter his room. Your object is for him to fall asleep alone. On subsequent nights, as shown below, you increase the amount of time that you let him cry before returning to his room.

If, after your child gets to sleep, he later wakes up and cries, start the process again, beginning with the minimum waiting time listed for that day. Continue this routine each time he wakes up, until getting-up time if necessary. The chart presents a seven-day plan, but the problem is often solved in less time than that. You can adjust the lengths of the waiting periods to suit yourself. Just remember that the periods must get progressively longer on any given night, and that the first waiting period each night should be longer than the first one the night before.

— Richard Ferber, M.D.
Director, Center for Pediatric Sleep Disorders
The Children's Hospital, Boston.

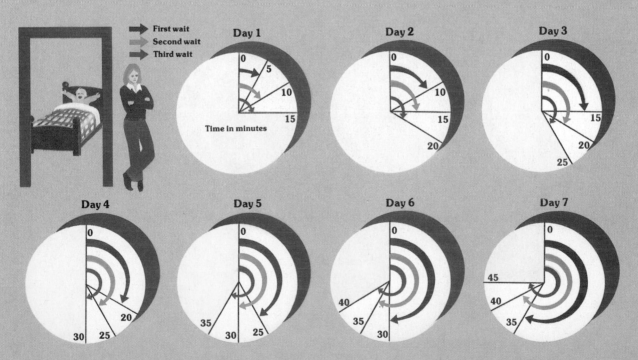

This chart displays in graphic form a program for training your child to go to sleep independently. The arrows indicate the amount of time you let the youngster cry before making a brief visit to the bedroom. The time that you should wait before returning to the child's bedroom increases after each *visit, until a maximum period is reached for that particular night. And the waiting periods lengthen for each successive night. If your youngster's sleep problem is still not solved at the end of a week's time, keep trying, adding five minutes to each waiting period each night.*

Early Sexual Awareness

As a parent, you play a critical role in your child's sexual development and adjustment. Your influence goes far beyond the traditional concept of sex education, in countless subtle ways, from the tone of your talk to the type of toys you buy, you help shape your child's attitude toward her own sexuality and that of others.

Sexual identity   During the first two years of life, as your child begins to explore her own body and to notice sexual differences, your actions and reactions will help her form a healthy sexual identity. As early as their first year, children begin to wonder why they are made the way they are. Their tentative explorations provide the first awareness of their bodies as a source of pleasure; before long, they learn that touching or rubbing their genitals creates feelings of excitement. Parental acceptance of this early behavior is important. For your child, the romantic fantasies and fixations of adult sexuality do not exist; her sexual exploration and experience reflect nothing more than a natural curiosity and healthy delight in her body. If her hand is angrily slapped away from her genitals, the toddler feels that there is something bad or forbidden about a part of her body — a part that, to her, is no different from her nose or toe.

During the second year, the toddler's growing awareness of differences between males and females sets the stage for the establishment of her own sexual identity. Increasing contact with siblings and playmates, coupled with the uncovering of body parts previously hidden under diapers, leads the toddler to a truly exciting discovery: Although children look pretty much alike with their clothes on, they are made in two distinctly different ways. This realization leads to close identification with the parent of the same sex. The little girl, observing that she resembles her mother, strives to be as much like her female parent as she can. The little boy, noticing that he has the same parts as his father, is eager to imitate him in every possible way.

Fascinating as these discoveries of similarities and differences can be, they sometimes cause anxieties in young minds. A little girl may silently wonder why she does not have a penis like her brother. A little boy may feel anxious about the obvious differences in size between his own body parts and those of his father. Parents can relieve such anxieties by clearly explaining sexual differences. Tell the toddler that boys and girls are made differently from the beginning; no one is missing any parts, and no one is going to lose the parts they already have. Emphasize the positive aspects of each child's gender, pointing out that boys can become fathers, and girls can become mothers, when they are older.

Roles and stereotypes   Sex roles tell children what types of behavior are acceptable for their gender. Unlike gender, however, sex roles are not irrevocably molded. Adults may share or exchange roles such as breadwinner, housekeeper and nurturer, depending on their age and culture. And during childhood, toddlers experiment with, and even reverse, sexual roles before reaching a healthy norm. Providing models for a child's sexual behavior used to be simple: Boys imitated their fathers and girls followed their mothers. Nowadays, parents must compete with outside influences,

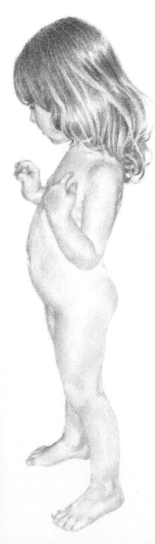

from the peer pressures of preschools to the appeal of television. At the same time, many parents have abandoned the rigid concepts of role — or stereotypes — that encouraged assertive, aggressive behavior only in boys, while ascribing passive, dependent roles to girls.

In guiding your child through this confusing and controversial stage, remember that rigidly-enforced stereotypes can damage your child's emotional and sexual development. While boys will be boys and girls will be girls, parents should recognize that both genders encompass shades of masculinity and femininity. In their attempts to learn who they really are, boys may play with dolls and pretend to have babies, while girls may favor trucks and act out the parts of fathers. Such role-switching play is perfectly normal at the toddler stage and should not be interpreted as a sign of sexual confusion or maladjustment.

Allow your toddler to experiment, while at the same time helping her understand clearly that she belongs to one sex. You can reinforce your child's gender identity and still react positively to cross-gender play. If your two-year-old son is bathing a doll, do not assume that he is playing at being a mother; instead, praise him for being a considerate daddy.

Usually children's experimentation with sex roles will diminish around the age of three. Regardless of how they play, make sure to instill in your little ones the feeling that you value them for the individuals they are, whether male or female.

The preschool and kindergarten years are often an emotionally trying phase of sexual development. As part of the natural effort to understand what it means to be male or female, a child predictably forms an intense attachment to the parent of the opposite sex and a confusing love-hate relationship with the same-sex parent during this time.

Such behavior usually begins around the age of three, as the child's strengthening identity and self-confidence instill a new sense of omnipotence. The little girl feels that she can do anything her mother does, while the little boy thinks he can do everything his father does. The sense of omnipotence may become so overpowering that the child secretly desires to take the place of the parent of the same sex. Under this childish spell, the boy's attachment to his mother increases; he wants to have her all to himself and wishes his father out of the way. He may announce that he is going to marry his mother when he grows up. The girl develops similarly possessive feelings toward her father.

While these childhood fantasies are ultimately harmless, they create tensions and anxiety in the child. The boy still loves his father and realizes that he needs his protection — even as he is rejecting him as a rival. Such tensions often lead to unpredictable outbursts of obnoxious behavior and stubborn defiance of the same-sex parent. Child psychologists also point to these conflicts as the cause of frightful nightmares in which animals and monsters chase the anxious child.

Parents can ease the tensions of this transition in several ways. First, you should recognize that it is a normal and necessary stage of sexual development. Gauge your reactions accordingly; remember that your

Answering Questions about Sex

Sex education may begin in your family as soon as your child starts posing such time-honored questions as, "Where do babies come from?" Let the questions themselves be your guide as to what, and how much, information your little one is ready to hear. Even when you tailor your reply to her queries, remember that not everything will be absorbed at once; expect to repeat your explanations, adding more details as the child grows older. And the best way to discover and deal with your child's preconceptions is to begin by asking her, "What do you think?" or "How do you think it works?"

The examples given here suggest simple but accurate explanations for the complicated questions children commonly ask.

Q. Why am I different from him?
A. Because you are a girl and he is a boy. Boys and girls are made differently.
Q. Why don't I have a penis?
A. Only boys have a penis. Girls are born with a vagina.
Q. Why are boys and girls different?
A. So that when they grow up, boys can be fathers and girls can be mothers.
Q. Where do babies come from?
A. A baby grows in a special place, called a uterus, in its mother's body.
Q. How does the baby get inside its mother's body?
A. The baby grows from a tiny cell, called an ovum, that was inside her body all the time.

child needs your love and support even if he appears to be rejecting your affection. Above all, do nothing to encourage these fantasies. The kindest response is to explain firmly and patiently that children cannot marry their parents; while you appreciate the child's affection, you already have a spouse, and a special grown-up relationship with him.

Your reaffirmation of your own parental role and relationship will help your child resolve his conflicting emotions. By the age of five or six, children come to accept their place in the family hierarchy. If he cannot replace his father, the boy decides, then he will be like him, and the girl aspires to be like her mother. The normal and healthy outcome of this phase is a strengthening of masculinity in boys and femininity in girls, and an increased identification with the same-sex parent.

Parents as teachers
As your child's sexual curiosity increases, she will turn to you for answers. Whether you welcome this role or not, your responses to her questions *(box, above)* will reveal not only what you want her to know but your own values and attitudes as well. If you fail to provide answers, she will get them elsewhere; more often than not, she will also get them wrong. In dealing with your child's inquiries, remember that she is interested in reproduction, not grown-up sexual feelings. It is best to label anatomical parts correctly from the start; changing from the familiar to the formal name later adds unnecessary confusion. Avoid confusing your child, as well, by giving her more information than she asks for. Answer her questions promptly and briefly, and let her ask for repetition or clarification when she is ready. Finally, avoid farming and gardening analogies in your explanations. Children associate eggs and seeds with eating, leading them to imaginative but erroneous jumbles of the digestive and reproductive systems.

Curiosity and privacy
As you strive for a balance between society's sexual norms and your youngster's natural curiosity, make sure not to shame or punish childish exploration. When your child innocently touches himself or plays with

Q. Who tells the baby to start growing?
A. When a mother and father want to have a baby, a cell from the father's body, called a sperm, joins the cell from the mother's body and the baby starts growing.
Q. Where does the father's cell come from?
A. The father's body makes a fluid called semen, with lots of tiny sperm cells.
Q. How does the father's cell get inside the mother?
A. The semen comes out the father's penis. The penis fits into the mother's vagina.
Q. Can I make a baby?
A. When you are grown-up like your mother, you can.
Q. Can I make a baby in you?
A. No, you have to be grown-up to make babies. Then there will be someone your own age to be the mother of your children.
Q. When do you make babies?
A. Mothers and fathers pick a time when they are alone together. Making babies is private.
Q. How does a baby get out?
A. When it is ready to be born, the mother's body gets a signal and pushes the baby out. The doctor helps it to be born.
Q. Where does a baby get out?
A. When a baby is fully grown, the mother's vagina stretches to let the baby pass through.
Q. Did it hurt when I was born?
A. Sometimes it did. When a baby is born, the mother has to work to push the baby out. But I was so glad to see you that I quickly forgot all about the hard work.

his genitals in public, try to distract him with a game or a story. Then matter-of-factly explain that touching his penis is private — something not done in public. When sex play involves other children, the situation becomes more complicated and emotionally charged. Few parents remain composed upon discovering their three-year-old son playing doctor with the little girl next door. While shaming would be purely destructive, you should not allow this type of play to continue, either. Children's curiosity is basically harmless, but youngsters also sense that this approach to uncovering mysteries is improper, and their explorations are mingled with anxiety and discomfort. They will be secretly grateful when you suggest that they get dressed and switch to a different game. Explain that while it is natural for them to be curious, you would prefer that they seek answers from you.

Children are curious about adults, too. But at an early age they are not emotionally prepared to handle excessive exposure to adult nudity and sexuality. While an occasional glimpse of unclad parents is not cause for concern, frequent exposure to parental nudity is disturbing for young children, who may find the experience secretly exciting and feel guilty about their reactions. Take particular care that your child does not interrupt sexual intercourse. Children are likely to misinterpret it as physical or verbal violence and conclude that their parents are hurting each other. If you do forget to lock your bedroom door, do not punish your child's curiosity. Instead, ask that he leave the room while you get dressed, then sit down with him and respond to any concern he may show. You may wish to explain that sexual relations are so private that not even members of the same family are allowed to share in them.

The respect for sexual privacy should be mutual. As your child approaches school age, he is apt to become suddenly modest and to show his own desire for privacy while dressing and bathing. Whenever such feelings develop, honor them matter-of-factly and accept them as one more sign of your child's progress toward sexual maturity. ❖

Fears and Fantasies

For the first few years of life, children's thought processes resemble those of our primitive ancestors: Youngsters are powerfully affected by invisible feelings and ephemeral images, but they cannot understand where these sensations come from. With their limited knowledge, young children find just about everything around them potentially scary. Until their mental abilities have matured enough to distinguish the real from the unreal, the external from the internal, youngsters are naturally susceptible to some degree of confusion and distress.

A child's imaginative life begins to quicken around the time he turns two, a result of his newly acquired ability to create independent ideas on his own. Suddenly the youngster is the possessor of an entire kingdom of images that exist solely within his mind: Side by side with the external realities of feeding and dressing, of riding in the car and playing with toys, the child now is contending daily with such illusory complexities as bears under his bed, monsters that chase him in his sleep and "friends" that are visible to him alone. At the same time, the child is struggling to sort out an inner world of intense feelings. Strong impulses that he will one day know by such names as jealousy and love and anger now strike him only as powerful sensations over which he has no control. These and other emotions, half-formed and only vaguely understood, blend with fantasy to create a host of fears and anxieties.

Baffling as such developments may be to parents, this age of flourishing imagination is essential to a child's well-being. Unfettered fantasy is the magical language of childhood: It helps the youngster adjust to the demands and frustrations of the real world by sheltering him from it. More importantly, it gives him the daring to explore. And imagining what can be is the first step toward true creativity — that uniquely human gift that your child will carry with him always.

Understanding Your Child's Fears

Fears big and small are a universal fact of early childhood — probably unavoidable even for the securest of children. Your youngster may voice anxieties as farfetched as "Are monsters real, Mommy?" or as logical as "Will the doctor give me a shot?" The thing to remember is that any worry, however silly it may seem to a grownup, can be quite real and utterly daunting to a young child. As you offer your youngster reassurance and comfort at such times, you should try to do so without using the words "There's nothing to be afraid of." To the child, there certainly is.

Many common childhood fears, such as the fear of strangers and fear of the toilet, result from developmental changes and therefore appear at certain ages *(chart, pages 80-81)*. These fears wax and wane and sometimes reappear at later stages, but in general, children simply outgrow them. By and large, if you let your child know that strong and loving adults are watching out for his welfare, this will provide the security he needs to overcome the passing fears of childhood.

Why children have fears

All human beings feel fear at times; it is an innate reaction to potential danger, part of the human instinct for survival. And because babies and young children are so dependent on others for their security, they are prone to many more fears than adults.

A child expresses certain basic kinds of fear long before she can talk. An infant, for example, will startle or cry when she hears a loud noise or feels like she is falling. As children grow older, more complex anxieties arise naturally from rapid changes in their emotional make-up and their expanding perception of the world around them.

Children's interest in their environment increases as they enter their second year of life, but their feeling of security is easily shaken by new experiences. They may be particularly skittish about sudden, unfamiliar sounds, such as the vacuum cleaner, passing fire engines or a barking dog. During the toddler stage, a child's fears seem to grow more ill-founded rather than less so. Partly this is because of her immature sense of spatial relationships and the child's distorted sense of her own size in relation to the size of the things around her. The youngster may display a fear of the toilet or the bath that is based on a concern about somehow being sucked down the drain.

The role of imagination

But the main reason for an increase in irrational fears after 18 months is the child's awakening imagination, which begins to intermingle with such emotions as anger and jealousy. These strong feelings often find expression in fears of imaginary enemies, such as robbers, monsters and bogeymen. The toddler may refuse to stay in a room by himself, or he may demand that objects like scary masks or stuffed animals be put somewhere out of sight.

Fears arising from his imagination reach a peak between the ages of three and five. Struggling to distinguish between real and make-believe, children of this age often invent fantastic explanations for things they

Scary Places, Scary Faces

❝ When Michael was about two and a half we were shopping in a small local store one day and the storekeeper was dangling his keys and jokingly said, 'Michael, I'm going to lock you in.' Well, within a day or two, the child would not go into any store with me. I couldn't take him anywhere at all, because he would not go into any place that had a door. No amount of reassurance would help at all. One Sunday, my husband and I took Michael with a bag of lollipops to the store and my husband carried him in and gave him lollipop after lollipop. Michael was really frightened to death, but we held on. We bought two items, checked out and left. We did this several weeks in a row, each time staying a bit longer. He finally realized that he wasn't going to be locked in. But that was a long ordeal. ❞

❝ One night not long ago it was the moon. Emily was eating dinner and all of a sudden she looked startled and said 'Scared!' When I asked her why she was scared, she said, 'Moon, the moon.' She does it just like that, everything will be fine and all of a sudden she'll say 'Scared!' and come running to me. It seems to be momentary. I'll tell her Mommy's here, Daddy's here, and then she repeats, 'Mommy's here, Daddy's here, baby's here' — meaning her little doll. That seems to reassure her. ❞

❝ I took Alex to the museum when he was three and a half, and when he saw the museum guard, he suddenly turned around and walked in the other direction. He thought it was a policeman and told me, 'Policemen shoot bad people.' He was afraid he might do something bad in front of the policeman and get shot. I showed him that the guard didn't even have a gun, and I explained about 'bad' boys versus really bad people like bank robbers. That lessened his fear of policemen, but he is still fascinated with them. ❞

❝ When he was two, Jonathan was terrified of clowns. At a carnival once, he spotted a clown and made a mad dash trying to reach me. En route he fell down, and who should stoop down to help him but the clown! He was hysterical, cried for about 15 minutes even after the clown went away. Six months later, he reacted the same way to the clowns in a parade. We told him that clowns are nice and make children laugh, but he kept saying, 'They're coming to get me, Mommy, I know it!' ❞

❝ When she was a baby, crawling rather than walking, Cara just hated grass. She wouldn't touch it. Lots of kids like to roll in the grass, but she was afraid of it — she hated the prickly feeling, I guess. She wouldn't go into the backyard and when we brought her there she wouldn't move, she'd just sit there and cry. She'd grab onto us, even if we set her down on a blanket, because she knew she couldn't get off the blanket without having to go through the grass. ❞

❝ Bennett's nursery had curtains with zoo animals all over them — a purple rhinocerous, a blue tiger and so on. When he turned two he started saying he was scared of the bears. We figured it was the curtains, so we took them down. But at bedtime he was still afraid. We'd have to go into his room and open all the closets and look under the crib and show him there were no bears. Gradually he grew out of it. But we never did put the curtains back up. ❞

do not understand, and in the process, they may assign human feelings and motives to inanimate objects.

In the movie *The Wizard of Oz,* an apple tree gets angry and hits Dorothy when she picks an apple. A scarecrow talks with a lion and a mean lady turns into a witch. To a three-year-old, all this is quite believable. And because of a young child's egocentric view of the world — his tendency to see himself as the pivotal player in every event — he imagines how all this might affect him. It may be a natural step for him to go from watching the movie fantasy to worrying that a witch or a tree might attack him in his own backyard.

The Common Fears of Childhood

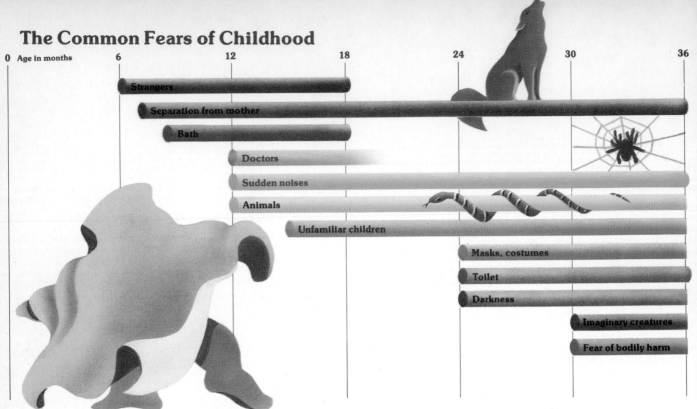

0 Age in months	6	12	18	24	30	36

Strangers

Separation from mother

Bath

Doctors

Sudden noises

Animals

Unfamiliar children

Masks, costumes

Toilet

Darkness

Imaginary creatures

Fear of bodily harm

Children also acquire fears through experience. A child who has been stung by a bee may fear all insects, just as one who can remember a painful inoculation may cringe at the mere mention of the doctor's office. Fears can be triggered as well by abrupt changes in the family situation, such as the birth of a new sister or brother, or the divorce of the parents.

From your perspective as an adult, it is not always easy to anticipate the impact of the things that your child sees and hears. Realistic scenes of violence on television are a case in point. A preschooler who laughs in delight as Saturday morning cartoon characters get flattened and "ker-boomed" might react quite differently to a dramatized gun battle between humans or to news coverage of a car bombing. The child might jump to the conclusion that such live-action disasters could happen to him. As you think about appropriate viewing guidelines for your family, remember that the moving images and dramatic sounds of television make it an extremely vivid medium for a small child.

Occasionally, even the words and expressions you use in casual conversation may spark fears in your child, whose grasp of the language is not as sophisticated as yours. When you offhandedly say "My boss is going to kill me," your youngster might take the statement at face value and start to worry that your life is really in danger.

How children cope with fears

Despite their vulnerability to fears, children may develop a surprising array of psychological strategies for dealing with their own anxieties. You may notice your youngster, for example, going through a super-hero phase of pretend play between the ages of three and five, when imagined fears tend to proliferate. Constantly reminded of their smallness and lack of control over events, children of this age often play the all-powerful hero in their fantasy games as a way of fending off the fantasy villains that threaten them.

Other children try to overcome fears by experimenting with the

The colored bars on the chart above indicate the ages at which common childhood fears most often occur. These are just the norms, however. A child may experience these anxieties before or after the age spans shown. As the chart suggests, the fears of an infant or toddler are usually reactions to real and immediate events, while a preschooler's fears more often stem from the child's imagination.

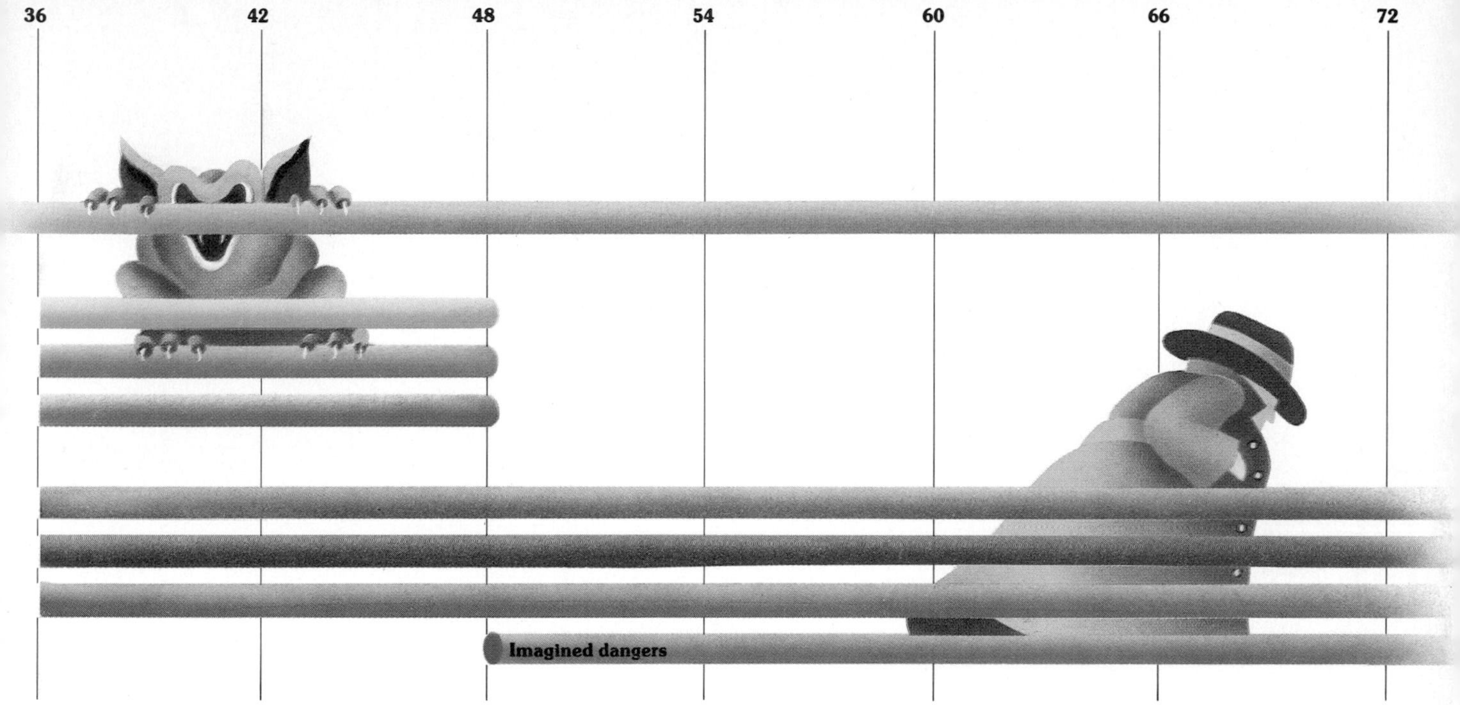

source. For example, a child who is fearful of being flushed down the toilet may try to flush a toy down the drain. Mommy may find it annoying to have to retrieve a sopping wet toy from the toilet bowl, but the child's reaction is quite the opposite: he feels reassured to see that the toy does not really disappear.

A youngster may also become quite strongly attracted to an object that he once feared, in an instinctive attempt to desensitize himself. If he was afraid of dogs, the child may suddenly stop to admire every dog that he sees. And many children use rituals as a method of holding their fears in check. A child who grows anxious and upset at the approach of bedtime is often comforted by a familiar routine — listening to a story, brushing teeth, then being tucked in and kissed goodnight — because it reinforces his sense of security.

Fear of strangers

A threatened sense of security, in fact, underlies many childhood fears. A child's first predictable anxiety — a fear of strangers — surfaces midway through her first year. Before this time, a baby will smile at anyone. But by about six months, her mental development enables her to distinguish between familiar and unfamiliar faces. Because the unfamiliar ones tend to leave her confused and uncertain, she may cry or try to hide her face when a stranger — even a close relative — approaches. The best way to minimize this fear is to expose your child early on to a variety of people.

Another security-related fear that arises at about this time is the child's fear of being left by her parents — a development often referred to as "separation anxiety" or "separation protest." It begins around the age of seven months, at first as a simple mental awareness that a familiar parental figure has disappeared from the scene. Later expressions of separation anxiety are more related to the child's deepening emotional attachment to her parents: Distress at being apart from these primary suppliers of love and security, even for brief periods, usually emerges at around 18 months and may continue until the child is three years of age *(page 100).*

Fear of the bath

Fear of taking a bath often appears late in a youngster's second year — a baffling development to parents of children who previously loved bath-time. The child's fear may be related to slipping in the tub, getting soap in his eyes or to a concern about disappearing down the drain along with the bath water.

If you are not certain what caused this fear in your youngster, try putting a rubber mat in the tub, using less water and not emptying the tub until your child has gotten out and left the bathroom. Also, demonstrate for the child that his bath toys cannot fit down the drain, and assure him that neither can he.

Fear of animals

Children sometimes develop a fear of animals while they are learning to walk. The sudden noises and unpredictable movements of a family pet are understandably disconcerting to a child not yet steady on her feet. She may also simply shrink away from animals that are unfamiliar or bigger than she is — especially if she has ever felt personally threatened by an animal. And if you are afraid of animals yourself, there is a good chance that your child will sense your fear and share it.

Usually, a child's fear of animals will pass by the age of three or four, barring scary experiences. You can help by reading stories about animals or by exposing your child to small, docile species while teaching her the proper way to handle them.

Fear of the dark

Fear of the dark is extremely common. It usually emerges between the ages of two and three, and though it typically diminishes by school age, it can last throughout childhood. This fear is normally related to the child's fantasies about monsters and other scary creatures, or to a wariness about nightmares or being alone.

The best approach is to acknowledge your child's fear and leave on a night light. You can also try to foster positive feelings about sleep by developing a comforting bedtime routine *(pages 68-69).* If your child's fear of the dark is extreme, you may on occasion have to sit with the child until she is calm enough to fall asleep.

Fear of school

The fear of going off to school usually arises from a child's anxiety about separating from his mother or father and facing unfamiliar teachers and children. Sometimes the younster's worries are reinforced by unpleasant experiences at school — a teacher who seems threatening, toileting accidents, aggressive classmates. In some instances, the fears can actually bring on stomachaches or headaches that keep the child from attending school.

School anxiety is usually overcome by the child's natural curiosity and eagerness to learn about the world beyond his home. However, this is an area where you as a parent need to be especially aware of your own

What to Do When Your Child Is Afraid

- Respect the child's fear as real. Never tease or berate your child for being afraid. Provide comfort and reassurance. Let your youngster know that you love him and will protect him from any real dangers.

- At the same time, do not inadvertently reinforce a child's fears by taking them too seriously. Indulging a youngster too much in this way can undermine her self-confidence and may lead to dependency.

- Do not force the child to confront the source of his fears. Rather, help him to investigate in nonthreatening ways. If he fears a monster in the closet, inspect the closet yourself while the child watches from a safe distance.

- Encourage your child to talk about his fear. Sometimes a simple conversation will help.

- Help your child dream up imaginary cures for imaginary fears. You might suggest, for example, "I'll bet we can invent a magical rhyme that will scare away that imaginary witch."

- Emphasize constructive action to make her feel less helpless. If your child fantasizes a disaster such as the house catching fire, go over the steps that you both would take in that event — for example, running outside and going to a neighbor's house to call the fire department.

- Set an example of calm in frightening situations. If you panic during a thunderstorm, chances are your child will, too.

- Read children's books with your child that deal with his fears. Ask your librarian to help you find good ones.

- Monitor your child's television viewing and pay attention to the kinds of books and magazines that she is exposed to.

- Do not confuse hesitation with fear. Children are naturally reticent in unfamiliar situations. Allow your child to go at her own pace. Praise her when she is brave.

feelings and the signals that you are sending your youngster. If you tend to be overprotective or have mixed emotions about your child leaving the home, as many parents do, his negative feelings may be an unconscious echo of your own.

Fear of bodily injury
Besides their natural aversion to pain, children have a tendency to internalize things they see, and this can lead to a fear of bodily injury. For example, a child who sees a physically handicapped person may worry that the same thing will happen to him. Some children feel particularly vulnerable during the preschool years, as they move out of the self-centered complacency of toddlerhood toward a more realistic awareness of their dependent place in the world and their less-than-all-powerful bodies. In this so-called Band-Aid stage, they often become preoccupied with minor scrapes and scratches and panic at the sight of blood. This anxiety usually passes by the age of five, when children become more comfortable in their role as children.

When fears become cause for concern
In extreme cases, a child's fears may be so intense that they interfere with his daily activities. A youngster who has an obsessive fear of insects, for example, may balk at going outside and can make life difficult for himself and the entire family. If common sense tells you that your child's fear is unusually severe or long-lived, then it is time to seek professional help for this problem.

For the most part, however, you will find that young children's fears are as fleeting as they are varied. You can help your child to be less fearful generally by encouraging him to be as independent as his age and his abilities allow. It is only natural to want to protect your youngster against potential dangers and frightening situations, but keep in mind that children need opportunities to develop a sense of competence and self-reliance. Meeting their fears head on gives them that kind of opportunity.

Eventually, experience is the child's greatest weapon against fear. He learns that though his parents leave him, or a jackhammer startles him, or shadows play on his bedroom wall, in the end nothing bad really happens to him at all. ❖

Dreams and Nightmares

Dreams and nightmares loom larger in a child's emotional life than in an adult's. The reason is simple: Young children need more sleep than older people do, so they have more time to dream. Moreover, children may be confused and disturbed by their earliest dreams — which are isolated images quite unlike the complex pageants of grownups' dreams — because they cannot understand where these images come from. To a three-year-old, a dream experience may seem as real as anything that happens in daytime life.

While the great majority of a youngster's dream images are pleasant or at least neutral in feeling, it is perfectly natural for him to suffer an occasional nightmare whenever the normal stresses of growing up spill over from his waking hours. It is these few unpleasant experiences — scary dreams of monsters and other threats — that will usually demand your attention in the middle of the night.

You may also have to see your child through a rather unusual sleep disturbance called a night terror, during which the youngster may appear to be wide awake and reacting fearfully to a nightmare, but in fact is still deeply asleep and unaware of what is happening. These midsleep dramas aside, most young children are able to take their dream adventures in stride.

The dreaming stage of sleep

In addition to sleeping longer hours, children up to the age of five spend a proportionately large amount of their sleeping time in the light stage of slumber known as REM sleep — named for the "rapid eye movement" beneath closed lids that characterizes the stage. This is the part of the sleep cycle in which most dreaming occurs, as opposed to the deeper, non-REM stage. Newborns spend up to half of their sleep time in the REM state, with the proportion of REM sleep decreasing gradually as the child grows older.

Much remains to be understood about children's dreams. In fact, no one knows for sure whether infants and very young children really have dreams at all, since children under the age of two do not have sufficient language skills to describe such experiences. Signs that infants experience REM sleep are obvious: They twitch their eyes, kick their feet, suck, smile and grimace in slumber. Some experts argue that this is not necessarily proof of dreaming. They speculate that the child's brain, like a computer running a program, is simply rehearsing reflexes for actions

like sucking, smiling, or moving the arms and legs. Others believe that the REM-sleep activities are indeed physical reactions to primitive dreams about sensory experiences.

What is clear is that when a child first begins dreaming, bits and pieces of recollected dream images lap over into her daytime consciousness and become mixed up with real experiences. Consequently, your preschooler may ask questions about unfamiliar people and events that you cannot possibly answer, because they refer to things that took place in her dreams. These seemingly nonsensical questions may be the first clue parents have that their child has indeed begun to dream.

How children's dreams evolve

The nature of a child's dream life generally mirrors his overall pattern of mental and emotional development throughout the early years. True dreaming seems to begin between the ages of 18 and 24 months, after the child develops the ability to form mental images. If you could enter the world of your toddler's dreams, you would find it a rather one-dimensional place, visited here and there by static images of the things the child has seen during the day. You might see animals — most likely farm animals or small species such as monkeys, squirrels and birds. Researchers studying the dream experiences of youngsters three years of age and older speculate that young children portray themselves as such animals in their dreams because they cannot yet envision their self-portraits in human form — and, perhaps, because they identify with the impulsive behavior of small creatures they see out-of-doors. At this stage, too, children's dreams frequently appear to be influenced by physical states such as thirst, hunger or fatigue, which may combine with animal imagery to produce dreams of small creatures drinking, eating or sleeping.

Early dreams involve very little dramatic or social interaction, and the settings are vague and nondescript. But as children reach the age of five or six, their dreams become more sophisticated, in parallel with their mental development. Story lines grow more complex and are less influenced by the child's bodily states. Now when a child dreams about food, the eating takes place in a social context. Animals still appear frequently — sometimes dressing and behaving as people — but family members are portrayed as well, and there is increased interaction between the characters in a child's dreams. The faces of strangers, sometimes frightening ones, may also appear in the dreams of a five-year-old. Researchers believe that these may simply be failed attempts at constructing more familiar characters. Recreation and play are dominant themes, and settings are more specific: Buildings and landscapes that are a part of the child's waking life now appear in dreams.

Nightmares

Although nightmares represent only a small percentage of children's dreams, they may seem more prevalent than is actually the case if they frighten your young sleeper into waking, crying and rousing the entire household. Researchers believe that all children have bad dreams, probably beginning in their second year, but that the earliest such dreams

are infrequent and very simple. A two-year-old, for example, may relive a frightening experience such as getting stung by a bee.

Nightmares are more commonly experienced by children from three to six years of age. Fevers and certain types of medication sometimes provoke scary dreams, but in most cases nightmares are brought on by the fears and other normal emotional concerns that arise from the developmental changes of early childhood. For example, a three-year-old child struggling with newfound feelings of anger and aggression may project these negative feelings as frightening imaginary monsters that threaten him in dreams.

Certain stressful experiences can cause daytime feelings of jealousy and rebellion that may surface during sleep as nightmares. A youngster who has a new brother or sister may find that his hostile feelings toward the baby are turned in upon himself in his dreams. He may envision being chased by someone big and threatening, or being left alone by the side of a desolate highway. These nightmares seem utterly real to children and often cause them to awake in a panic.

It rarely will soothe a child to tell her that a nightmare was not real or that it was only a dream. Real or not, it genuinely frightened your child, and she needs your sympathy and support. The best thing you can do is to hold her close and talk to her in a calm, reassuring tone of voice. Let the youngster know that you will always take care of her and protect her. Stay with her if she is afraid to go to sleep. It is not wise to make a habit of lying down with the child or taking her to your bed. But sometimes a story, favorite toy or simply a night light will help the youngster get back to sleep.

With older children, it sometimes helps to talk about the dream the day after. You might encourage a five- or six-year-old child to act out the drama and to think of ways to overcome the things that frightened her. Though this may not alleviate the specific fear that caused the bad dream, it may reduce the child's anxiety about nightmares.

If disturbances persist

Some children have more nightmares than others, and frequency of bad dreams is not necessarily cause for alarm. It is not unusual for a child to experience nightmares for several nights in a row, followed by several nights of calm sleep. But recurrent nightmares may indicate that the youngster is having difficulty adjusting to a trauma, such as an accident, or to stress in the family. One other possibility to consider is a medical condition called apnea, in which the child's breathing is interrupted, causing him to awake frequently. The disorientation and fright that accompany this wakening may easily be confused with a nightmare. If your child has prolonged and repeated nightmares, you should consult your physician.

Night terrors

Night terrors are much less common than nightmares and are often mistaken for bad dreams, although the two experiences are quite different *(box, right)*. The name "night terrors" is somewhat misleading, since the child will not always be terrified. He may scream or thrash about, but he may also talk quite calmly, sleepwalk or just stare into space. Parents frequently describe their child as looking possessed during such an episode. Because night terrors occur in the deepest stage of non-REM sleep, the youngster never fully wakes up even if he becomes very agitated.

Night terrors tend to run in families. Researchers believe that they are related to quirks in a child's awakening mechanism: Instead of shifting smoothly from deepest non-REM sleep to the dream state of REM, the child partially rouses. But night terrors do happen more often when a youngster is very tired, so their occurrence can also tell you that your child needs more sleep.

One of the real problems in helping a child who is having night terrors is that it is not always obvious just what is happening. You may be groggy yourself and assume that the youngster is simply distraught from a nightmare. Keep in mind that night terrors most often occur in the first four hours of bedtime, when the child is most tired and spends more time in the deeper stages of sleep. Nightmares generally occur in the latter half of the sleep period, especially in the hours near dawn when REM sleep prevails.

All you can really do for night terrors is make sure that the child does not hurt herself. Remove toys from the floor around her bed so that she does not trip if she sleepwalks. Do not try to wake the child up. That will usually just agitate her more and prolong the episode. If she wants to be held or comforted, then do so, but do not force your help on her. After a brief period, she will simply settle back to sleep. ⁝

How to Tell Nightmares from Night Terrors

Nightmares

- Frightening dreams take place in light sleep, often awakening the child.

- You become aware that the child is troubled after the dream is over.

- The child will appear to be very frightened, perhaps crying if he is very young, and he may be difficult to calm. The youngster will probably be reluctant to go back to sleep.

- The child is reassured by your presence and may cling to you.

- The scary dream is often remembered by the child the following day.

Night Terrors

- The child partially rouses from very deep sleep. Dreaming is not involved.

- You will be aware of the child's terror while it is happening.

- The child usually seems confused and may cry out, talk or moan. She may sit up, stand, thrash about or sleepwalk. Bulging eyes and sweating may also occur. The youngster will settle quickly back to sleep.

- The child may seem oblivious to your presence or angrily push you away.

- She will not recall the episode but may seem vaguely anxious the next day.

Fantasy and Imagination

Children of any age may enjoy an elaborate fantasy life as a normal and healthy part of their development, but fantasy plays a particularly vital role in the years between two and five. Almost any exercise in imagination — whether it is pretend play, humor, an imaginary friend, a tall tale or even an outright lie — may, at bottom, be part of the child's effort to understand the world and learn how to behave. Remember that there is a big difference in the way you see reality and the way a young child sees it: Toddlers and preschoolers are still learning to distinguish between what is real and what they have imagined.

Most of your child's fantasies will be make-believe games. The child feeds a toy bear with an empty spoon or dresses up and marches off "to work." But you may also see pretend behavior that is disturbingly aggressive. What do you do when your child spins out yarns about murdering the new baby? And you will definitely see behavior that, while not disturbing, is perplexing and demands a response. How should you react when your little girl keeps shooting you with a banana? Should you be concerned when your little boy prefers to dress up like Mama or jokes endlessly about "poo-poo"? Strange as it may seem, any of this behavior may be part of your child's learning process.

When imagination develops

Babies are not born with fully developed powers of imagination. In the infant and early toddler stages, their understanding of the world is based solely on direct interaction with the people and things around them. Then, usually at about 18 months, a child develops the ability to form mental images and, as her vocabulary expands, to give these images names. Now that she is able to link her knowledge to symbols — to create and name a mental image of a boat and how it works, for example — the child begins to combine objects and ideas in creative ways. She uses one object to represent another: A bar of soap floating in the bath becomes a boat crossing a pond. Emotions, too, come into play. The child imagines a doll as a new baby to be fed and loved.

Fantasy becomes the child's tool for exploring the adult world and, by trial and error, for finding a place in that world. The child is constantly seeking ways to assimilate new experiences into her picture of reality. Confused by the differences between male and female, a little girl may announce that she is a boy and try to sample life from that perspective. Troubled by feelings of anger or aggression, a boy may shout "Bang! Bang!" and lure his father into a make-believe fight. Imagination also provides the opportunity to fulfill a wish, to be in control or just to hold onto good feelings for a while longer.

The uses of pretend play

The most common form of childhood fantasy is pretend play. A child's first attempts at pretending are usually simple imitation. At about 15 to 18 months, the child may "drink" from an empty cup or pretend to go to sleep. But once he is able to use symbols in his thinking, the youngster may pretend there is a cup when none exists or pretend to lay a doll down to sleep.

Between two and three years old, your child will begin to build make-believe games around real experiences such as shopping trips and tele-

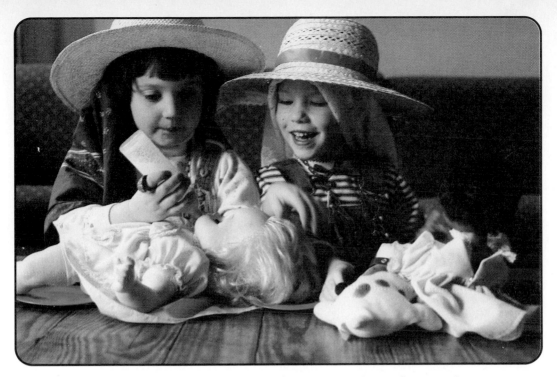

phone conversations. At this age, children are exploring their sexual identities. If you see your child alternate between male and female roles, do not be alarmed. Many children experiment in this way to learn what sex differences mean. Beyond the age of three, the child begins to identify more strongly with the parent of the same sex and most often emulates that role.

By the age of five or six, the child is more interested in people outside the home, and you will see the role playing become more realistic and complex. Now a number of characters may take part in the same story. Police, firemen, ambulance drivers and helicopter pilots may all be called in to help in an imagined disaster.

Pretend play will often focus on your child's awareness of his place in the world. Children have little control over their lives, yet their desire for control is great. By playing superhero, monster or wizard, your child creates a scene where he is the master. By acting the part of a school crossing guard, the child gets to tell Mom and Dad when to stop. Children crave such reversals.

Youngsters also use pretend play to help them understand troubling experiences. When a new sibling arrives, for example, watch your older child's play for clues about feelings. She may express anger and jealousy by scolding or spanking a doll — or by throwing it across the room. The child probably knows that she could never treat the baby that way. But acting out a fantasy like this releases built-up tension and lets a child find out how it feels to give way to emotions. It is probably best not to interfere at such a moment. But afterward, ask the child to talk about what is bothering her, and sympathetically explain the reality of the situation if it is something — like a new baby — that cannot be changed.

Unpleasant memories and fears can sometimes be mastered through fantasy. Children who are frightened by animals or who develop a fear of doctors sometimes switch roles and pretend to be the object of their fears. By assuming an active role in the drama and replaying real or imaginary scenes, the child takes control of the situation. You can encourage such play by providing the props — puppets, dolls, a toy doctor's kit or some fanciful clothes to dress up in.

A child's humor
Pretend play also helps in less serious matters. By finding humor in play, a child releases tension and reclaims that elusive sense of personal power. Your child probably loves to catch you making a silly mistake. For a moment, she can feel smarter than you. In the same vein, a child delights in mimicking your authoritative voice and manner. Even just acting silly herself — making mistakes on purpose, falling down or pretending to be clumsy — can allow the child to feel more in control.

Two other subjects that many children like to laugh about are sexual differences and bathroom matters. This kind of humor may drive you to distraction, but it seems to help relieve a child's anxieties about these issues. In egging each other on to yet another toilet joke, children find a sense of camaraderie among peers sharing the same uncertain feelings. And by finding amusement in a subject that began as a worry, the child learns a lesson in optimism.

Storytelling skills
Like other forms of fantasy, children's stories reflect their experiences, fears, emotions and desires. Your two- or three-year-old may attempt to tell a story using phrases and short sentences, but he can only sustain it with much questioning and prompting from you.

By the age of four, your child will pick up conventional storytelling devices such as "Once upon a time" and "the end," and he may become more fluent in telling a tale. This age is the imaginative peak for children's stories. The action is seldom bound by reality, and the story settings may be wildly exotic. You can encourage storytelling by reading to your child regularly. New characters, situations and locations from books become fuel for his own stories.

While the plots of young children's tales often involve eating, sleeping and the appearance of a kindly figure, violence is far and away the predominant theme. You are likely to hear a great deal about struggles with monsters, children getting spanked, stolen food, death, killing and crashing. Although such stories may make you rather uncomfortable, remember that they are usually a child's way of dealing with fears or feelings of aggression. And they give you a perfect opportunity to talk through such concerns with your youngster as the two of you discuss the gorier details of the story line.

Tall tales   During this period, a child's stories may take on the characteristics of a tall tale. The child will claim to have accomplished an incredible feat — she rode her tricycle a million miles. If challenged, she may indignantly proclaim that it is not just a story, it is true. There is usually no harm in just acknowledging the story and letting it go at that. At times you might gently interject some reality — it may not have been a million miles on the trike, but it was farther than yesterday. This lets her know you understand her tale and that you take it for what it is worth.

Sometimes, however, your child may tell what you consider to be an outright lie. Here again, you will often need to exercise restraint. "Lie" is too strong a word for the transparent fibs that a small child tells. Children generally fib only to protect themselves from punishment and, since the line between fantasy and reality is so easily blurred, your child may actually believe she was not at fault. In dealing with this type of behavior, it is usually more constructive to forgo punishment and instead to talk with the child, emphasizing your appreciation for honesty. In this way you will teach her that she has little to fear in taking responsibility for her actions.

Imaginary friends   When called to account for being naughty, some children pass the blame on to an imaginary playmate. The existence of such a "friend" may come as a surprise to you, but be assured that it is quite normal for children between the ages of two and five to invent such companions. The child may imagine the playmate as another child, an adult, an animal, or even a favorite toy or blanket come to life. It is not clear why some children have these friends while others do not. In most cases, the child is aware at some level that the friend is only pretend. Unless your child becomes dependent on an imaginary companion to the exclusion of human relationships, do not worry. If it reaches that point, however, ask your pediatrician for advice.

Children assign many roles to imaginary playmates, and by paying close attention to the reported antics and pronouncements of such a character, you may gain some insight into your child's state of mind. Sometimes the playmate provides an emotional outlet, voicing fears or hostilities for the child. Other playmates do naughty things that test parental limits, allowing the child to watch Mother's reaction from a safe distance. For the child who is trying to learn self-control, an imaginary playmate may serve as a Jiminy Cricket-like conscience. And in many cases the character is nothing more than a reliable companion.

For you, however, an imaginary friend may be more of an exercise in patience. Usually the best strategy is to accept your child's fantasy without encouraging it. Let her know that you realize the friend is make-believe and that you understand the fun of pretending. Punishing your child or ridiculing her fantasy may only encourage her to hide the companion. Imaginary friends are generally developed to fulfill a particular need. When that need is satisfied, the playmate will disappear. Like other expressions of the child's imagination, a fantasy friend helps her explore new territory along the path to emotional maturity. ⁖

The Feelings Revealed in Children's Art

For 35 years, children's art specialist Sylvia Feinburg has been collecting the art of young children and using it to explore the interior world of childhood feelings. Her collection, sampled on these pages, shows the amazing range of information about a child's state of mind that the youngster's art can yield.

Painting and drawing come as naturally to young children as speaking. The act of guiding a crayon or paintbrush across paper not only is fun, it is a satisfying means of self-expression as well. Art lets children communicate feelings their limited vocabulary cannot convey — hopes and fears, pleasures and anxieties and opinions. But the messages, as in all art, are given in code and may be hard to decipher.

A picture's real meaning often lies beyond its subject matter and technique. Young children tend to draw the same things — houses, trees, people, vehicles, animals, the sun — and to draw in similar ways. They also typically exaggerate and distort, producing bodies with limbs too long or fingers too numerous.

Generally, the best guide to a picture's meaning is the child's own commentary. The remarks here were prompted by questions from the teachers in whose classes the drawings were made. Significantly, the questions were never as direct as "What are you drawing?" or "Is this a house?" — but rather, "Would you like to tell me something about this painting?" Children who decline such invitations to explain, however, should never be pushed. It is far more important to let a child enjoy the immediate pleasure of creation than to discover what the picture may mean.

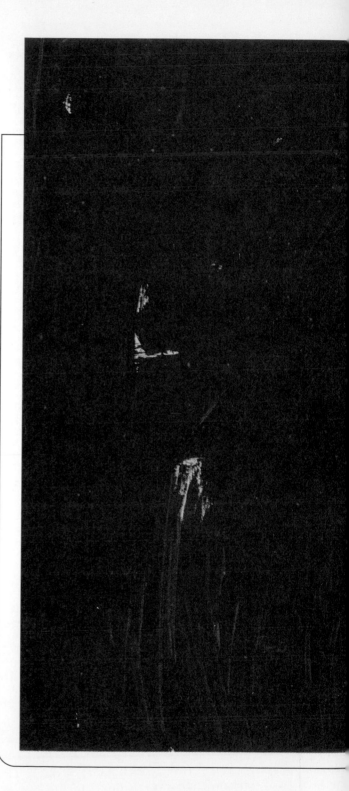

In drawings, children often transfer their feelings to animals: "The mother cat with babies at her nipples," explained the four-year-old creator. "The other cat is telling the baby cats to drink their milk from a bowl." The witty picture suggests a typical case of sibling rivalry spurred by a new baby's monopoly on a mother's attention.

A haunting image — described by its maker as "me watching television all alone in the house at night" — illustrates the nearly universal childhood fear of abandonment. Whether or not this particular event ever took place, the child's portrayal of a small figure enveloped by darkness signals anxiety about the possibility of its occurring — and thus a need for parental reassurance.

"Now I'm four but someday I'll drive a car," announced the creator of this picture. For many young children, cars, trains and planes symbolize power and competence, and their frequent appearance in drawings is associated with aspirations to these qualities.

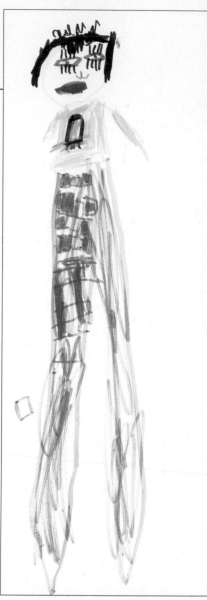

"I'm a nice girl because I'm not naughty. I think about nice pictures and nice designs," said this kindergarten pupil, describing herself. The self-portrait's harmonious colors and rosebud mouth seem to mirror the child's preoccupation with pleasing adults.

"I am a person inside a girl, a plain girl. I like to think about people dying. I like to go to birthday parties. I like to go down to the store." This jaunty child embellished her "plain" portrait with bold brushstrokes and capped it with a litany of random thoughts typical of a five-year-old.

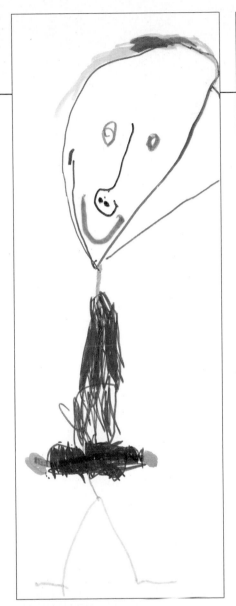

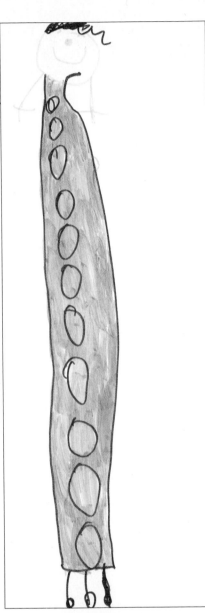

"I am one of the smartest boys in the class. I have lots of good ideas. I am sometimes happy and sometimes sad . . . happy when happy things happen to me, sad when people tell secrets." A self-portrait that is mostly head reflects this youngster's awareness of his high intelligence.

"I am an American person, shorter than this room and taller than this picture," said this young artist. "Bones and blood and ribs are inside of me." Obviously intrigued by his physical make-up and size, the child gave himself a string-bean body accentuated by a row of 11 buttons.

"I look different from other people. I do different things from other people." As if to underscore his individuality, this child drew a portrait unlike his classmates' simpler scenes: He enclosed his in a fancy border and decorated it with a background of earth, clouds and smiling sun.

"There is a big lion trying to come into the house," explained the painter of this forbidding image. "If he catches me he'll take me home and eat me for dinner." Less alarming than it may seem, the painting was prompted by a classroom activity designed to help children distinguish between dreams and reality. Monsters are common five-year-old fantasies, and not necessarily cause for concern.

"A strange creature came down and he made all the houses go up in the air except for me and then he made all the trees go up except for three. That's all." With this lyrical description of a dream, coupled with an equally lyrical — and finely organized — painting of trees and houses afloat in space, the young artist illustrated how illusion and reality often blend in dream logic.

Times of Special Stress

All parents want their children to be happy and care-free, protected from the world's hurts and disappointments. But events sometimes turn the lives of children topsy-turvy in ways that leave them baffled, uneasy, perhaps deeply troubled.

These disturbances, as discussed on the following pages, may range from such seemingly innocuous situations as moving to a new house to serious occurrences like divorce or the death of someone the child loves. Children are hit particularly hard by such events because they involve loss and change, two experiences that threaten the security youngsters derive from stable and routine living patterns.

Another factor disturbing to the child is lack of control over what is happening. It is the parents, not the child, who decide whether to move, whether to have another baby, whether to divorce. No one consults the child about these important decisions. She is left feeling helpless in addition to feeling upset.

Doubtless the parents, too, are distracted and worried by the same problems at the same time, in some cases coping with emotions even more intense than those the child experiences. Nonetheless, caring parents will try to ease the pain and reduce the damage these crises can inflict. By understanding the emotional effects of such events and showing your child how to deal with them, you will help prepare him for the inevitable future disappointments and tragedies of life. Learning to survive a negative experience will make your child stronger.

Separation from Parents

Whether you are going back to work or just going out for the evening, at some time you will need to leave your child in another person's care. The prospect of spending even a brief period away from the emotional security provided by parents may provoke in young children a disturbing feeling called separation anxiety. These early separations can be an ordeal for parents as well, as any mother who has pulled a crying, clinging toddler off her leg can tell you.

If the experience leaves you feeling guilty, you may draw some comfort from the knowledge that your child's behavior is commonplace, reenacted daily at thousands of schools, homes and day-care centers, and that countless children have survived the stress of separation anxiety to grow into happy and productive adults. You should also know that you can reduce the stress for everyone involved by preparing in advance for your youngster's feelings and reactions, which vary according to the child's age.

The age when anxiety begins

Until he is five or six months old, your baby probably will not protest when you leave. Content as long as their needs are met, such young babies are not choosy about who takes care of them. For this reason, some mothers who are going back to work deliberately plan their return for these early months, even if it is much sooner than they would like.

By seven to 10 months of age, however, the infant has developed an intense attachment to her parents. She is aware of their absence when they are gone and begins to feel upset when she sees them leave. So when you walk away, even if only to go into the next room, the child feels abandoned and may cry. The simple act of going to sleep can become a problem, because sleep means parting from you. In addition, the taste of independence that comes with a newfound ability to walk brings with it a sense of aloneness that can be scary. So while a little one may dash off to explore the world, she frequently runs back to her parents for security and reassurance.

Reactions of toddlers

It is not until after the age of two that a child begins to understand that the parent who leaves will also return. While this may somewhat ease the child's panic about your departure, it will not entirely alleviate the problem. At this age, the child is eager to control the world, and may feel angry and a little frightened when he can't prevent your going.

But as children grow older they acquire an understanding of the reasons for separations, and the anxiety diminishes. They begin to enjoy the prospect of playing with other children and exploring new surroundings. This does not mean you must be with your child constantly until he is three or four. There are things you can do to ease his transition at any age to a substitute caregiver. The first thing is to find someone you trust to fill that role.

Selecting a caregiver

Finding a first-rate sitter or day-care center is often difficult, but the caregiver you choose can make a big difference in your child's adjustment to being separated from you. If you have serious doubts about the care you have chosen, your child will sense your reluctance to leave and will resist your going. If, on the other hand, you feel good about the new arrangement, she will respond to your confidence.

As you consider the credentials, training and reliability of prospective caregivers, also ask them how they would help your child to cope with separation anxiety. Some believe in ignoring or trying to suppress your child's tears and complaints about your leaving, when in fact it is much more helpful for the child to vent her emotions. Acknowledging her need to cry and complain is a way of showing the youngster that her feelings are legitimate and she is respected, and a wise caregiver will understand this. Once you have made your choice, provide the caregiver with your child's complete daily schedule and a list of her particular likes and dislikes. Convey as much as you can of your child's individuality — the words and phrases she knows, how actively she gets around, the manual skills she has mastered. This information will keep disruption of your child's life to a minimum and will help the caregiver encourage her social and emotional growth.

Preparing your child for parting

Even before your child is a year old, there are ways you can begin preparing him for being apart from you. Playing games that involve disappearing, like peekaboo and hide-and-seek, will show him that absence can be temporary and that the lost can be found. Another useful game consists of your leaving the room for a short time while maintaining voice contact. Return periodically to cuddle and play with the child, gradually lengthening the time you stay out of sight. This kind of play can help a baby understand that you continue to exist — and continue to think about him — even when he cannot see you.

Make sure that your child will have as few additional stresses as possible at the time you plan to first leave him. His start in day care, nursery school or with a new sitter should not coincide with weaning, toilet training or the birth of a sibling.

If your child is old enough to understand — at least 16 months or so — talk to him ahead of time about an approaching separation. With

How to Say Good-by to Your Child

- Try to make leave-taking brief but unhurried. If your child is able to understand, tell him a few minutes ahead of time that you will be leaving soon.

- Tell your child when you will return for her. Explain this in a way she can relate to: "I'll be back at suppertime."

- Don't try to stop your child from crying or expressing unhappiness in other ways when you leave. Such expressions are important for the child. Accept his protests sympathetically, and offer reassurance that you will return later. Remember that his crying is likely to end as soon as you leave.

- Be sure to make it clear throughout the parting process that you are definitely leaving. Your calm and certainty will help your child accept the separation. If you show that you are upset, she will intensify her protests.

- Encourage your child to wave good-by through the window once you are outside. This second good-by will give him a sense of control. Other departure routines, such as his bringing you your pocketbook or hat, may be helpful in the same way.

- Any departure ritual may ease the transition, whether that ritual is a special good-by game, a song you sing together, or a set routine of removing outdoor clothes and beginning play. Like bedtime rituals, departure routines reassure your child at an anxious moment. But be warned: Once adopted, they can be altered only at your peril.

very young children who have little concept of time, however, explanations are best reserved until shortly before it is time to part. Gear them to your child's level of understanding, telling him in as much detail as possible where you will be, who will be looking after him and what he will be doing. Explain why you must leave him behind, answering all of his questions, even if he asks the same ones repeatedly. And always assure him that you will think about him and still love him while you are away and that he can count on you to come back to him again.

Introducing the caregiver

If your child is six or seven months or older, and someone is going to care for her in your own home, ask the sitter to come for several visits first. As the two of you chat in a relaxed and easy manner, the child will observe your confidence and may even try to make friends with the sitter. When your child seems comfortable with the sitter, stay a few minutes, then leave for a short time. The next time, you can stay away longer; it may take a week of visits before a child is willing to spend an entire day with the sitter.

If your child will be staying in the sitter's home or at a day-care center, visit the new place with her ahead of time — making sure to take along her favorite security object. Your goal is for her to become familiar enough with the new setting so that its strangeness does not pose an added problem for her when you leave. Introduce her to the caregiver and, at a day-care center, to some of the other children. Point out toys to play with. Then withdraw to a discreet distance where you can remain available while letting the caregiver take the lead. By being nearby but not participating, you will direct your child's attention and trust away from yourself and toward the caregiver. After several visits, stay for an hour or so and then leave for a while. Once your child has learned from experience that she can manage without you, and that you do come back, she will be able to accept a longer separation.

Leaving   When it is time for you to leave, always say good-bye *(box, opposite).* Slipping out unseen might be easier for you, but it would make it difficult for your child to trust you in the future. When your child realizes you are departing, she probably will feel anxious and begin to cry. Try to remain calm and reassuring, and not hesitant about leaving, since she can sense any doubt on your part. Keep in mind that the moment you leave is usually the most distressing one for the child, that within minutes she is likely to forget her tears. If you need reassurance, call the caregiver during the day to check that all is well.

Eventually, children adjust to baby-sitters or day care, although they may continue to protest tearfully when their mothers leave. But even a child who is obviously contented with her sitter or day-care center will react with fresh anxiety if the arrangement is changed. Switching from being looked after at home to attending a center or school requires an especially big adjustment. When any change is necessary, plan on helping your child to adjust once again.

The reunion   You may envision a warm and loving reunion after a day away from your small child. Unfortunately, the reality is sometimes very different. He may be delighted to see you and eager to talk about his day, or he may be excessively clingy and babyish. But it is also possible that he will greet you with an icy stare and cold shoulder, as if showing lingering resentment about your earlier departure. Some children become very angry and may even try to bite or hit their parents.

Such ill-tempered behavior is difficult to take when you are tired and concerned about getting lunch or dinner on the table, but you must remember that your child, too, is tired, and ready to release any pent-up emotions of the day. After so many hours away from you, he will crave and need your attention, and you will want to find a way to give it to him. Planning ahead for the transition time when you reunite with your child is helpful. Give him your undivided attention when you first arrive; talking with the caregiver can wait a few minutes. Some of the pressure may be relieved if you bring snacks for your child and yourself and if you explain to other family members that dinner will not be ready as early as they may hope — unless they are willing to prepare it!

If your child is angry or unhappy, listen as patiently as you can and let him know that you understand how he feels. If he is in a negative or indifferent mood, persist in wooing him back again. But if he becomes violent or destructive, make it clear that, though you love him, you will not tolerate such behavior.

Once he has settled down, talk with him about his day and about yours. Focus on the enjoyable things he did in your absence and on the fact that you came back as promised. Try not to make your time away from him sound too exciting, and remind him that whenever you go away, you will come back.

Like most changes, first partings are painful. But they are a necessary step in your child's growth. Handled well, they will help him get ready to take his place in a large and demanding but exciting world. ∴

A New Baby Arrives

The birth of a sibling arouses in any child a tangle of feelings: curiosity, admiration and love, but also envy, resentment and outright jealousy. The younger the firstborn child, the greater her dependence on you and thus the stronger her reaction to the new competition. A child younger than three is likely to be very upset by the baby's arrival. Lacking the intellectual development to understand exactly what is going on, or to talk about and control her feelings, she may regress in behavior and could show her anger in physical ways. An older child who already has her own friends and a somewhat independent life may be mature enough to discuss her anger. But whatever your firstborn's age, she will probably feel hurt, because — in her mind — you have brought home a new child to take her place. You can take steps to minimize this, but there is not much you can do to eliminate it altogether.

How to break the news

If your firstborn is two or younger, hold off announcing the expected birth until the pregnancy is obvious. To toddlers, seven or eight months is an eternity to wait. The older your child, the sooner you should talk. Tell your five-year-old before you tell the neighbors; otherwise, you may yourself hear the news from your own child.

Make the announcement simple and direct — "We are having a new baby in the family" — conveying your excitement and enthusiasm. Resist saying, "We like you so much that we wanted to have another." After all, imagine how you would feel if your spouse informed you that you were so terrific the only thing to do was to acquire another just like you. Nor should you promise a baby brother or sister "to play with." Months and months will pass before the new baby can qualify as a playmate.

Getting ready

Once you announce the pregnancy, there are many little things you can say and do to head off your child's worries. Reassure him that although there will now be two kids in the family, you will love him as much as ever. Some youngsters think of love as a commodity like a candy bar. If you divide it, they believe, there is less for everyone. Do your best to dispel this idea. Refer to the expected child as "our" new baby. At baby showers, arrange for the older child to give the baby a gift, and make sure that the older child receives a gift, too. You can establish a spirit of camaraderie with your "big" boy or girl by talking about babies and the demands they make. Looking together at your older child's baby photographs will give both of you a loving moment to reminisce and forge stronger ties. If the new baby will be breast-fed, prepare your child for the sight in advance by letting him watch another mother nurse her infant.

Being as upbeat as possible, explain how the new sibling will affect your older child's life. Whatever else you do, avoid making any big changes in the child's routine, such as moving him from crib to bed or starting toilet training. Any move like that should be made long before you ever tell him about the new baby. Your child may ask questions about where the new baby comes from *(box, page 74)*. Answer these as straightforwardly as you can, but keep your explanations at a level the child can grasp.

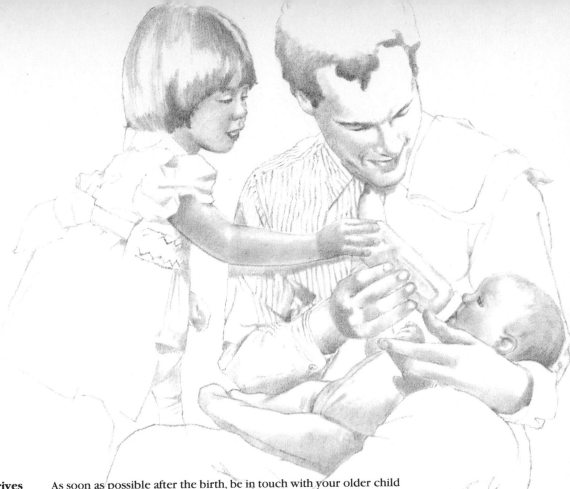

When the baby arrives   As soon as possible after the birth, be in touch with your older child by telephone. When she visits the hospital, spend time telling her how much you have missed her and asking about her activities.

On coming home from the hospital, again focus special attention on big brother or sister. You might plan to have Mother enter the house first alone, for an affectionate reunion with the older child, letting Father come behind with the newborn. In the following weeks, spend as much time as you can with your firstborn. With all the new demands on you, this will not be easy, but it is crucial to her sense of self-importance.

Try to get your child to discuss her feelings. If she tells you that she does not want the baby to stay, tell her that you understand, but remind her that the baby is a permanent member of the family. If she says that she wants the baby to go away or to die, simply comfort her and take her feelings in stride. A young child does not really comprehend death. She is just expressing her feeling of being displaced. Nonetheless, never leave the two of them alone. Toddlers have no concept of their own strength and may not understand that a baby is different from a toy.

A balancing act   Your baby and your older child are both individuals, and each should have some time with each parent every day. You may need to stagger naps or even hire a sitter now and then to be sure that each child gets his share of attention. Having specially arranged play-dates with friends shows your older child how grown-up he is compared with the baby.

As your child grasps that there is plenty of love to go around, he or she will begin to enjoy the new status of older sibling. And you, too, will increasingly cherish the special bond that grows between you and your firstborn — a relationship that you will never lose. ∵

Moving to a New Home

For a child, moving to a new home may be the end of the world. Do not be surprised if your announcement of moving elicits from a toddler or preschooler a sullen, nonnegotiable reply: "I won't go." For her, this denial is a normal way of dealing with the threatened disruption of her universe, centered as it is around a few familiar faces and places.

Younger children will not offer such opposition, although they can pose problems of a different nature. A very young infant may be fussy and difficult at moving time simply because she is responding to your own stress signals, such as muscle tension or abruptness in the way you deal with her. A crawling baby, older than six months or so, can make moving more complicated, because she is likely to be underfoot. Naptime is shorter, too, which means that you have fewer uninterrupted moments to pack.

Winning your child's enthusiasm

You can do much to ease the anxieties. If your child is old enough to understand, tell him about the move right away — before he learns about it from playmates or finds realtors poking through his closet. Explain the reasons for the move and acknowledge your own emotions. His fear of being lonely at the new place will seem less overwhelming if he senses that you are sharing it. Above all, if your child balks at the idea of leaving, do not respond with your own ultimatums. Instead, steer the conversation to the good things he is sure to discover in the neighborhood.

Gather information on your future community's parks and playgrounds, libraries and zoos, schools and day-care centers. If you cannot take your child to see the new home and community in advance, make photographs. Once he has at least a mental picture of where he is going, the move will make more sense to him. You can also play moving games with your child, using toy trucks and block houses and encouraging him to express his emotions.

Preparing for the move

With younger children, your task is not so much to win their enthusiasm as to keep them content and safe. If you have a very young infant, set aside a comfortable chair so that despite the chaos of packing, you and the baby can still enjoy feeding-times together. If yours is a crawling baby, pack medicines, cleaning compounds, and sharp or breakable objects while she is sleeping.

Through it all, maintain as normal a routine as the hustle and bustle will permit. Take breaks from the planning and packing to visit a favorite park. These interludes will benefit you as much as your child. And do not forget that your toddler or preschooler may want to take some special memories of the old neighborhood along. Make up a scrapbook or collage from pictures of her favorite haunts and playmates. This visual record will provide comforting reminiscences and a sense of continuity while she is still adjusting to her new world.

Moving day

Include your toddler or preschooler in the moving activities as much as possible. Sending him off to a relative may keep him out of harm's way, but being present will help him grasp the finality of moving. Have him pack his own toys and write his name on his boxes. The chores will keep him occupied and give him a stake in the move's success. Set aside a few treasured items — a stuffed animal or a favorite storybook — for the journey to your new home. In spite of your understandable urge to get rid of unwanted belongings, this is not a good time to discard even seldom-used toys. Children made insecure by moving may be suddenly possessive of every dismembered doll or rusted toy car. Throw them away only after your child is securely settled. And ask the movers to pack a large toy — a tricycle, for example — last on the van. When you arrive, it will be unloaded first, and your child can begin enjoying the new neighborhood right away.

Settling in   Involve your child in the process of moving in. Let her help arrange her room and unpack toys. Set up her room before any others, making her bed and putting her furniture in a comfortably familiar pattern. These reassuring surroundings will provide her a cozy refuge from the general chaos as you sort out other rooms.

But you should fight off the temptation to unpack and arrange the whole house at once. Instead, explore the new community with your child. Find the library, the park, the supermarket and, if one exists within reach, a toy store. And take advantage of the great excuse that children provide to meet the neighbors. The sooner you start knocking on doors, the faster your child — and you — will begin forming new friendships.

Initially, your child may feel particularly lonesome and vulnerable at bedtime, so postpone major changes in sleeping arrangements — switching a toddler from a crib to a bed or moving a preschooler from a shared bedroom to her own — until the family is more settled. Take time to read a favorite bedtime story as your child settles down for the night. And remember to leave a night light on, not only for reassurance but to prevent missteps in unfamiliar surroundings. Even so, your child may experience sleeplessness, restlessness or a sudden finickiness about food. These behavior changes will probably pass as she gets over the stresses of the move. Do not try to force the pace, but stand ready to smooth out rough spots along the way. With time and understanding, acceptance will turn to excitement as the possibilities of the present replace the memories of the past. Although moving may be the end of your child's world, remember that her world is built anew every morning. ❖

Going to the Hospital

Going into a hospital, even if only for a very short stay, can be an unsettling and frustrating experience for your child. After years (or months) of learning to do things as grownups do them, she suddenly may be required to sleep in a crib, to eat a baby-like diet, to wear an embarrassing hospital gown, to use a bedpan not unlike a baby's potty, and to endure poking with thermometers and needles. Children often view such procedures as punishment and feel guilty about being ill.

At worst, the hospital experience can be very frightening. Children under the age of four can be especially terrified at the thought of being separated from their parents. Older children may have an intense fear of being mutilated; to them, a tonsil may seem as vital as a tongue. Their fears may give rise to awful fantasies and misunderstandings. Doctors have reported young patients mis-hearing the word "edema" as "demon," interpreting "penicillin" as a threat to the penis and seeing a masked surgeon as an evil criminal.

Explanations that will help your child

You can ease your child's fears by explaining this strange place to him. Start by questioning your doctor and the hospital staff about the details of the planned hospital stay *(check list, opposite)*, so that you can confidently answer all your child's questions. Then matter-of-factly explain to your child why he is going to the hospital and tell him what to expect, concentrating on what could become alarming experiences, such as X-rays, anesthesia and drawing blood for tests.

Be more general about procedures that your child will not actually see, such as surgery. Say candidly what things will hurt and explain that, if they hurt too much, the doctor will stop the pain with drugs. Do not glorify the hospital or make promises that neither you nor the doctors can keep, such as a quick cure for a serious ailment. Explanations should be tailored to your child's age. Tell a toddler about the hospital one to three days before admission, a five-year-old a week or more beforehand. Bring up the subject bit by bit over several days, so that your child can take in the information without being overwhelmed. Picture books designed for the purpose or drawings that you make yourself can help with the explanations. You might encourage your child to play hospital, with himself as the doctor and a doll or stuffed animal as the patient; helping Teddy get well can convince a child that the doctor wishes to help him, the child, in the same way. And if possible, take your child on a tour of the pediatric ward before he is admitted.

Going into the hospital

Your child will badly need your physical presence and emotional support while she is in the hospital. If she is older than six or seven months, one family member should stay at her bedside day and night throughout a brief hospitalization, even if this means sleeping in an armchair or on a cot. Allow her to cry and voice her fears freely; this is not the time to ask your child to behave like an adult.

Offer to help the nurses with bedpans, dressings, baths and meals. Seeing you perform these tasks will assure the child that your role in her life has not changed. Whenever you must leave — for a cup of coffee,

What You Should Know Beforehand

Here are some questions to ask your doctor and the hospital staff in advance, so that you can explain the situation to your child:

● How long will your child be in the hospital?

● Can you stay overnight? If not, can you have 24-hour visiting privileges? When can siblings visit?

● What kind of room will your child be in? Must she sleep in a crib? Is there a TV? A phone?

● Will your child's diet be restricted? Can you bring food from home?

● Can your child wear her own pajamas? What toys or books can be brought from home?

● What tests and treatment procedures will the child undergo? Will they hurt? What sort of stitches, bandages or casts will be used?

● If surgery is required, what, if anything, can your child eat before the operation? What sort of anesthesia will be used? Can you stay with your child while it is administered and join him in the recovery room before he wakes up? What follow-up care is planned? What will the scar look like?

perhaps, or a trip home — say good-by and explain that you will return. Although she may cry more in your presence and during leave-takings than she would alone, these fusses are far better than the terrified withdrawal that might result if you abandoned her to the hospital. If surgery is required, try to arrange to hold your child's hand while anesthesia is administered and to be at her side when she wakes up.

Emotional aftereffects   In spite of all your efforts, your child may reveal confused feelings of anxiety, anger and betrayal after being hospitalized. Even though you pamper him, he may seek more attention by regressing to bed-wetting, thumb-sucking or feeding from a baby bottle. He may have trouble sleeping, suffer from nightmares or develop new, irrational fears — of the dark, strangers or separation from you.

He may blame you for the hospital ordeal — particularly if the convalescence is lengthy, since children often unconsciously expect an instant cure. He may show depression, throw tantrums or make bitter accusations aimed at you. The best way to handle such behavior is neither discipline nor overindulgence, but tolerance and reassurance. Encourage him to talk about his feelings and to reenact the hospital experience in play, which can help him change feelings of being a helpless victim to a sense of active control. When he is disobedient, gently affirm your long-standing rules. That will give him assurance that his family world is still in order.

Helping siblings through the crisis   Finally, do not forget your other children — particularly young ones — who may suddenly start behaving badly. A healthy sibling may blame herself for somehow causing the illness, or may feel neglected and resentfully demand more attention, or secretly may fear catching the illness. These troubles, too, can be eased by preparation. Before your sick child enters the hospital, explain the situation to the others. During the hospitalization, try to maintain a familiar home life, rather than sending the healthy youngsters to stay elsewhere, and encourage them to visit the sick one or to exchange notes, drawings and phone calls. Such activities can reduce the trauma for the whole family. •:•

When Parents Divorce

Nothing short of a death in the family, and sometimes not even that, can be more disturbing to children than the separation and divorce of their parents. How much damage a child suffers depends to a great extent on how the parents handle the situation. Of course, it is not easy to behave rationally when your own life is going through so powerful an emotional upheaval. But if you and your spouse can both keep your child's well-being uppermost in your minds and behave accordingly, you can reduce the pain and fear that your child will experience.

How to tell your child   Ideally, you and your spouse should sit down together to tell your child as soon as you are absolutely certain of your decision to separate. If one parent will not take part in this, the other will have to assume the responsibility. Any child old enough to be aware of what is happening and to take in a simple explanation — certainly any child of two years or so — needs to be told. Try to explain it to him in a way he will understand: "You know how much Daddy and I have been fighting, how angry we've been with each other. Now we've decided that we just can't live together anymore. It makes us too unhappy. But we both love you very much and we'll both still be your parents." However you choose your words, be positive. If you are indecisive, your child might latch onto a false hope that you will change your mind.

It is important to tell your child as much as he can understand about the practical details — where he will live, who will take care of him, when and how he will see the other parent. These are the questions he will be immediately anxious about. Do not burden him with your own bitter feelings. His self-esteem will be strengthened if he can grow up loving and respecting both his parents. You will not help him by saying bad things about your spouse, and you will only make it more difficult for your child if you ask him to choose sides.

Relieving the child of blame   Young children often have an egocentric view of the world and assume that they are somehow responsible for everything that happens. Silly as it may sound to an adult, a child might react to the news that her parents are separating by thinking it is because her father had to scold her for spilling her milk at dinner the night before.

This tendency to feel that they are at fault is particularly strong in children aged three to five, who often want to spend more time with the parent of the opposite sex. Boys of this age occasionally fantasize about getting rid of their fathers — and girls, their mothers — so that they can have the other parent all to themselves. The child may assume her jealous thoughts caused the separation and feel very guilty. Therefore, it is important to keep reassuring her that she is not to blame, and to encourage her to express her feelings and ask questions. You may have to bring up the subject several times before she will be ready to talk.

Typical reactions   Keep in mind that your child is mostly concerned with how the divorce affects her. She is apt to worry that if one parent is leaving, the other might eventually do the same. Ease her anxieties by reassuring her that she will be well cared for. And try not to feel hurt if she does not seem to sympathize with what you are going through. Some children

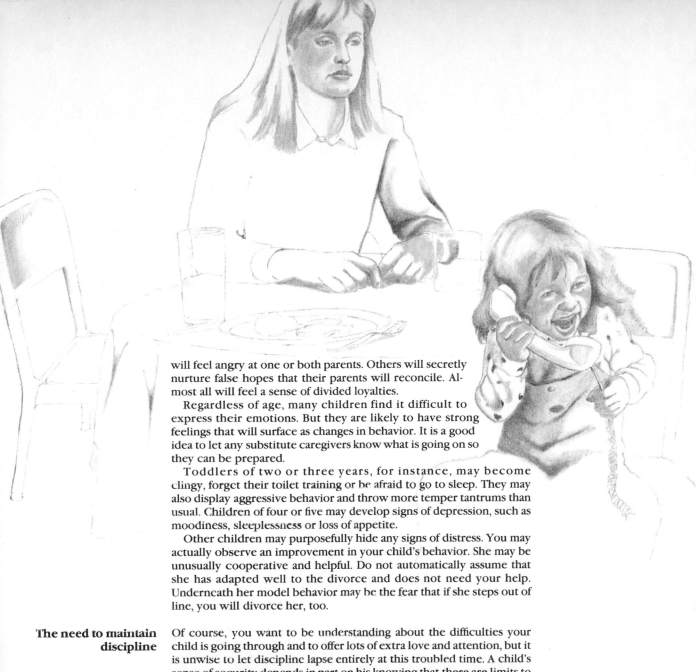

will feel angry at one or both parents. Others will secretly nurture false hopes that their parents will reconcile. Almost all will feel a sense of divided loyalties.

Regardless of age, many children find it difficult to express their emotions. But they are likely to have strong feelings that will surface as changes in behavior. It is a good idea to let any substitute caregivers know what is going on so they can be prepared.

Toddlers of two or three years, for instance, may become clingy, forget their toilet training or be afraid to go to sleep. They may also display aggressive behavior and throw more temper tantrums than usual. Children of four or five may develop signs of depression, such as moodiness, sleeplessness or loss of appetite.

Other children may purposefully hide any signs of distress. You may actually observe an improvement in your child's behavior. She may be unusually cooperative and helpful. Do not automatically assume that she has adapted well to the divorce and does not need your help. Underneath her model behavior may be the fear that if she steps out of line, you will divorce her, too.

The need to maintain discipline

Of course, you want to be understanding about the difficulties your child is going through and to offer lots of extra love and attention, but it is unwise to let discipline lapse entirely at this troubled time. A child's sense of security depends in part on his knowing that there are limits to what he can get away with and standards he must meet. Many parents become erratic about discipline after a separation or divorce, because they are caught up in their own problems and because they miss the decision-making help and the moral support of their former partner. It will benefit the child if you can overcome these difficulties and maintain a firm and steady, if gentle, disciplinary hand. It is particularly important for the two parents to agree on discipline standards and to enforce family rules evenly and consistently. Shuttling back and forth between a strict parent and a lenient one will only increase your child's sense of confusion at this unsettled time and may tempt him to favor the indulgent "good" parent over the "bad" disciplinarian.

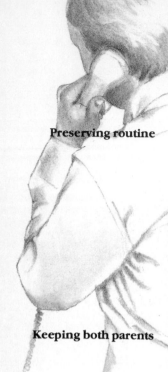

Preserving routine

In fact, anything you can do to keep your child's life as it was before the separation will help. Young children thrive on familiarity of surroundings and predictability of routine. Any change contributes to insecurity. The sudden absence of a parent from the home will be easier to take if your child still goes to bed in the same room and still goes off to the same play group or day-care center when he wakes up.

Such consistency after the breakup of the family may not be possible, for very good reasons. Newly reduced finances may require a move of residence or a change in daytime care. Perhaps a mother who has been caring for her child full time will now have to get a job; or she may need a job or a change of residence for purely emotional, but nonetheless very important, reasons. Only the individuals involved can decide such matters. Just keep in mind that any beneficial, established life patterns that can be kept in place will give your child something to hang onto as he tries to weather all the unavoidable changes.

Keeping both parents

The most valuable part of the former family life that a child can hang onto is easy access to both her parents. To maintain this bond despite the breakup takes the dedicated and diligent efforts of both parents. Of course this means that the parent who leaves the family home — in our society, by choice or by legal decree, this is usually the father — must try to stay close to the child, on a regular and intimate basis. But it also means that the custodial parent must take positive steps to maintain and support that relationship — no matter how much pride, anger and bitterness must be swallowed in the process.

Nothing short of clear-cut child abuse should be used as an excuse to keep child and parent apart. Blocking a spouse's access to a daughter or son hurts the youngster more than anyone else.

So important is the child's relationship to both parents that it is increasingly considered a good reason for joint custody. Sometimes this means the child shuttles at regular intervals from one household to another. In other cases — probably better for the child, but not for the parents — Mom and Dad move in and out while the child stays in place.

The nonresident parent

Much more common is the arrangement in which the child lives with one parent and visits, or is visited by, the other. If you are the nonresident parent, you must maintain regular contact with your child, even if only by telephone because you live so far away. Do not think he needs you any less just because you no longer live in the same house. Arrange regular times for your calls and visits, and try never to be late. For your child, this may appear to be a sign that you do not care.

If distance reduces your parenthood to phone conversations, make the best of the situation by planning, regularity and attentiveness. Call often, call on time, pay close attention, and ask questions that show how much you care. What did your child eat for breakfast? Does he like oatmeal now more than he used to? What is he going to do about that bully at the day-care center that he mentioned yesterday? If you do not see him very often, you may be tempted to make up for your absence from his life by showering him with presents and special outings to help make your experience together more pleasurable during the limited time you spend with him. But being a "weekend Santa" is not the same as being a good parent. You can maintain a more realistic relationship by setting limits on your child's expectations and imposing some responsibilities, such as asking him to help around the house.

When you have to be an only parent

If the other parent withdraws from your child's life, try to persuade him or her to return to the child. Explain sincerely how much the child misses and needs her other parent. If that does not work, appreciate that this is sadder for your child than for you. Let her know you understand how disappointing the absence of the other parent is for her. Help her recognize that it is not her fault.

Other special problems will arise. Because young children are establishing their sexual identities, it is especially important for them to have role models of the same sex. A parent is most frequently the child's role model, but if the parent is not available you should look for a suitable substitute in the person of a teacher, friend or relative who is willing to give time and attention to your child.

Children also need to develop positive attitudes toward members of the opposite sex. Obviously, it is difficult for them to do this if their parents frequently vent grievances against men or women. However angry your divorce has made you feel about the opposite gender, keep it to yourself and your adult friends, and make sure your child is well acquainted with some admirable adults of the opposite sex.

You may be tempted to turn your child into a friend and to share grown-up conversations and interests with him. Usually, this is unfair to the youngster. The best way to avoid it is to spend time with other adults and to pursue adult interests. Be prepared for your child to make your social life as a single person awkward. He will probably quiz you about your friends and activities and may ask some embarrassing questions. Answer his questions as honestly as possible. But, short of lying, keep the romantic details of any new relationship private. Overexposure to adult sexuality can be disturbing to young children, particularly those already unsettled by their parents' separation.

Help for the future

If adjusting to your new life becomes too difficult for you or your child, seek help from your doctor or minister, or from support groups such as Parents Without Partners. Many people report feeling more confused and doubtful about divorce a year later than immediately afterward.

While you should do what is best for your child during this difficult period, do not try to hide your own feelings. If you are depressed, it is better to acknowledge that "Mommy's not very happy today" than to leave him wondering what is wrong. And if he offers you a hug to cheer you up, be sure to tell him how much he means to you.

Try to be optimistic. If you are unhappy, it can affect not only your child's day-to-day spirits but eventually his outlook on life. The faster you can accept your changed situation and make up your mind to get on with your life, the better off your child will be. •ː•

A Parent's Remarriage

Although children may be genuinely delighted when they learn that a single parent is marrying again, it is almost inevitable that they will also feel powerful negative emotions — and the older the child, the more negative the reaction is likely to be, at least up to the age of six or so.

A very young infant may not be disturbed at all when someone new enters the family. But a baby old enough to know the difference between his parent and other adults may show some signs of stress: crying more, sleeping less, losing appetite, clinging to the familiar figure and rejecting the stepparent. A toddler of 18 months to about three years old can be expected to whine, cry and stage spectacular tantrums both to get attention and to drive away the rival for his parent's affections. Toddlers may also become more dependent, refuse to dress or feed themselves, and even forget their toilet training.

Children older than three will feel even sharper anxieties. The fear of losing love is particularly painful for a child who wishes to be especially close to the parent of the opposite sex, a behavior common in this age group. News of remarriage will also put an end to any hopes preschoolers may be nurturing that their natural parents will one day reunite. And children of this age are likely to worry, too, that by accepting a new stepparent they are betraying the absent biological parent. You can expect them repeatedly to challenge the stepparent with taunts like "You're not my daddy!"

Preparing your child for your new marriage

These negative reactions are completely natural, and you should not let them discourage you from taking a new mate. In the long run, a successful remarriage will increase the child's happiness as well as yours. You can help your child accept the change by introducing the new love in your life gradually. Children need time to adjust both to the possibility of a parent's remarrying and to the individual involved.

Once you have decided to marry, present the news in a positive way. Say how happy you are, and take care not to give the impression that your child can change your mind. Do not declare that you are acquiring a new mommy or daddy for her. Instead make it clear that your new spouse will not try to take the place of the absent parent, that the child and her natural parent will keep on loving and seeing each other just as before. You can underline this point by discussing what name the child wishes to call the stepparent. Explain what the new living arrangements will be, and if possible, avoid moving to a new home until your child has become used to the marriage.

Tips for a stepparent

The key for an adult dealing with new stepchildren is to move slowly. Avoid showering them with expensive gifts or physical displays of affection. But take care not to appear too stern or critical, either. Studies have shown that the most successful stepparents are those who act as adult friends of the child, firmly supporting the family rules, but leaving the job of primary disciplinarian to the natural parent.

Most important, as a stepparent do not be surprised to feel a confusing mix of emotions yourself: pleasure, frustration, love and anger. At

Living with Stepchildren

66 My three-year-old son David showed his opposition to my new marriage during the ceremony, which was outdoors. He marched into the middle of the guests and urinated on the lawn! At home he wouldn't cooperate when my husband, Steve, tried to help him dress, and he never wanted Steve to read to him at bedtime. David had a favorite fantasy: He wanted all of us to have an apartment with three bedrooms in a row. His father would have one room, Steve another, and David and I would share the middle room. When Steve's and my new baby came, David was four and a half. We were anxious about how he would feel and were delighted to find that he loved the baby and that it helped draw him closer to Steve. 99

66 I hate what being a stepmother brings out in me. I do all the things a mother does — laundry, cooking, carpooling — but sometimes my husband's boys behave so badly that I'm resentful and don't want to do anything for them. When they're with us I'm tense, I'm irritable, our sex life goes down the drain. I'm not blaming it all on them. My own son behaves terribly when they come. They are all so jealous and threatened by each other. People say it takes three

years to work through everybody's feelings in a remarriage with children. Well, we've been married three years and we've still got a long way to go. We'll make it through this because of the total love and trust my husband and I share. But I know it can never be easy. 99

66 The first time my husband's five-year-old twin daughters came to visit, Roz, the confronter, burst into our bedroom one morning. 'You're in my father's bed,' she said. 'Yes, I am,' I replied. She stood there staring, apparently waiting for me to vacate the bed. After a minute or so, she said: 'You're on the wrong side.' 'So I am,' I agreed, and I moved to the other side. That seemed to satisfy her, and it set the tone for our relationship: They could not rule their new stepmother, but she would bend when she could. 99

66 Being a stepparent is the most difficult thing I have ever done, even though I had lovely stepchildren: cute, funny and endearing, quick to learn and affectionate. They were also often obnoxious and demanding, moody, insolent, messy and expensive. Being a stepparent means you have to be grown-up. You may feel it is unfair that you have to put up with them, but you chose the situation; they didn't. I had to remind myself of that over and over. Now they have

become kindhearted, capable, well-adjusted young adults anyone would be proud to be related to. 99

66 Having had his mother to himself, three-year-old Eddie viewed me as unwelcome male competition. Every time I visited my bride-to-be, Grace, Eddie would hide. Grace's mother helped ease the situation by repeated reminders that 'Grace and Eddie are marrying Dick.' I managed to get him to come with me to buy our 'marrying suits' together. I knew he was warming toward me when Grace and I took him for a haircut a few days before the wedding. He jumped from the barber's chair eager to be my best man, but started wailing when he caught sight of his reflection. 'I wanted to look like Dick,' he sobbed. By the time he was five he was boasting to his classmates that he had the smartest dad in town. He meant me. 99

least part of the time you are almost certain to feel rejected, but you should try very hard not to answer rejection with rejection. Patience will pay off in the long run. Stepparents have an advantage in winning over infants and toddlers, who are still highly dependent on adults for their needs. With an older child, it may take two or more years to develop true trust, although with sensitive handling you can probably achieve a comfortable relationship — even a fun one — much sooner.

Special complications   Of course, forming a bond with a stepchild whom you see only on vacations or weekends can take longer. And mixing stepsiblings from different families into one household complicates all the relationships involved. In the latter case, rivalries are intense and bullying is common, making it extremely important for the adults to enforce rules fairly and to pay individual attention to each child's feelings and needs. ⁝

Bereavement

Children should not be shielded from an awareness of death. Loss is as much a part of young life as love and joy, and children who experience the death of a family member or even of a pet must be allowed to grieve.

The best way to prepare your child is to talk with her about death before it comes close to home. An autumn walk as dead leaves fall from the trees, the discovery of a dead bird or sighting a funeral procession, for example, provide opportunities to discuss the natural place of death in life, calmly and without the pain that accompanies personal loss.

The death of a pet Typically, children's first experience with death is when a pet dies. Even if it is only a goldfish, the loss may upset the child who cared for it. A parent's instinct may be to lessen the impact by running out to buy another fish. But coping with the death of a pet helps children prepare for other, harder deaths. Your handling of the situation can turn this loss into a learning experience. First, explain to your child that the death is final and let him know he is not to blame. Answer his questions and allow him to express his feelings. Encourage the practicing of a ritual, as basic as placing the dead animal in a box and burying it. Flushing a fish down the toilet may be easier, but children might think they, too, can be casually flushed away. For the same reason, replacing the pet right away is not wise. Explain that getting over the loss takes time.

Confronting the loss of a relative or friend When a loved one dies, tell the child about it in direct, honest and unambiguous terms. Say why the person died: "Grandpa's heart wore out." Explain that he will not return, that he can no longer eat, breathe, or think. Draw a clear distinction between any religious statement you make about the deceased's soul or afterlife and the physical being that is now dead. Describe how the body will be buried or cremated, assuring the child that the dead person cannot feel pain, heat or cold.

Children do not want philosophical explanations so much as reassurance that their parents will be around to care for them and that they themselves will be around to be cared for. If your child asks, "Are you going to die?" or "Am I going to die?" you can answer, "Yes, but not for a very, very long time." As you talk, use touch as well as words to convey that the child will continue to be cared for and protected. Hugging and caressing your youngster will help to allay the fears of abandonment that she will feel when someone important to her dies. And assure her that nothing she did or thought caused the death.

How children perceive death Your child's questions will give you clues as to what he is capable of comprehending. For example, a child under three years old typically perceives death as just another form of separation, and while he needs to be told that the missing person is dead, the finality of the event is beyond his imagining. What is meaningful and disturbing to a toddler is the disruption of routine. Everyone seems distracted. Grownups cry. Meals and nap schedules go by the board, and the youngster cannot get the attention he is used to. All of this threatens his sense of security. The best way to help the toddler is to restore his routines as quickly as possible, in an atmosphere that is consistent, loving and familiar.

Children older than two begin to have some understanding of the realities of death. Being dead, your three-year-old may tell you, is being "not alive," not able to move. She has probably stepped on enough bugs to establish that. Still, there tends to be confusion as to how permanent this condition is. When told that Daddy has died, a preschool child might be upset and saddened for a while, then dismiss the whole idea, waiting for her father to come home. Relating death with sickness, a preschooler may fear that others, including herself, will "catch" death. Only sometime after the age of six does the average child begin to be able to accept the notion that a particular person is irreversibly dead.

For these reasons, be careful not to explain death in confusing terms. Do not say Grandma has gone on "a long journey," for the youngster is likely to think that Grandma will come back one day, or that any trip can end as badly. By the same token, do not say that someone has "gone to sleep forever," as your child may become scared of going to bed.

Funerals   Unless your child clearly does not want to attend the funeral, it is probably best to include her. The solemn farewell ceremony will help to confirm the person's death, and it is a major family event in which the child, who now more than ever needs to feel important, is entitled to play a part. Describe what will happen during the service. If the body is to be in an open casket, prepare your child for what she will see and let her decide whether she wants to look. And be sure that someone she trusts stays close at hand to comfort her during the ceremony.

Grieving   Sometimes your child's reactions will not meet your expectations. He may show little or no sorrow. He may ask what seem to be callous or morbid questions, or might be insensitive to the feelings of others who are mourning in more traditional ways. But resist the temptation to manage his grieving. Do not insist that he display sorrow at the appropriate moments or, on the other hand, that he act brave and dry his tears. Rather, help him to talk about the deceased. Make him feel free to express his feelings. And do not simply dismiss his ideas, however unreasonable they may seem. Instead, explore them, guiding him to see his fantasies in a more realistic light. Most children, given sympathetic support, will come through the grieving process with their own spirit, as well as their memories of the loved one, alive and well. •:•

An Expert's View

When to Seek Professional Help

When a close relative or friend dies, a child may manifest grief in the ways noted below. In mild form, these reactions are to be expected, and the child's pediatrician can help with the problem. But if one or more of these grieving behaviors becomes intense and persists for six months or so — or if the grief is so extreme that the child cannot function normally for any period of time — then the pediatrician may suggest consulting a mental health professional. Here are the signs to look for:

● Denial of the reality of death. The child keeps expecting the dead person to return.

● Physical distress. The child is listless, grumpy, tired and achy and has stomach pains.

● Panic. The child worries about being abandoned. He may demonstrate this fear by being constantly demanding, throwing tantrums, bed-wetting and clinging to his parents.

● Guilt. The child blames herself for the death — particularly so if she has lost a sibling or parent. She may show the guilt feelings in depression or in angry, aggressive behavior.

● Apathy. Shows no interest in play and may refuse to eat.

● Hostility. The child is angry with the dead person for abandoning her. She may turn the hostility onto others, being stubborn, aggressive, perhaps hitting or biting.

— Benjamin S. Siegel, M.D.
Associate Professor of Pediatrics
Boston University School of Medicine

A Child's Development from Birth to Six

The development of a happy child proceeds in logical, predictable stages marked by breakthroughs every bit as meaningful as the baby's first steps or first word. By describing the milestones your child will pass as she learns about herself, her feelings and her relationship with the world, the chart on the following pages will enable you to recognize each new stage in this evolution and to encourage your child's growth in confidence and social ease. But keep in mind that many areas of emotional development cannot be speeded up at all, because they depend on the child's overall maturation and on related developments in three key areas: mental ability, use of language, and muscle control. For that reason, the sequence and pace of progress in these three areas are also included in the chart.

The chart divides the first three years of life into six-month increments and then covers ages three to six, a period when change comes less rapidly, in one-year time blocks. The developments within each section are listed in the order in which they usually happen — although some stages occur so nearly simultaneously that it is impossible to say for sure which will start first or go on the longest. The ages noted in the chart are only averages. Every child develops at a different rate, and the process is subject to fits and starts, a spurt of growth often followed by a plateau or even a temporary regression. Do not be concerned if your child appears to be developing at a more leisurely pace than the chart indicates. However, if you observe that your child is lagging significantly behind the age noted in a particular area of growth, you may wish to consult your pediatrician, if only for reassurance that all is well.

Birth to Six Months

Emotional and Social

- From birth, cries to attract attention when distressed.
- Enjoys physical contact, when held, stops crying.
- Follows moving object or person with eyes.
- Quiets to a comforting face or voice.
- By around 2 months, recognizes parents by sight, smell and other senses.
- Watches people, concentrating on their faces and eyes.
- Sucks thumb, fingers or fist to reduce tension.

- At about 4 months, laughs aloud in interactive play.
- Soon greets familiar people by reaching out to them.
- Draws attention to self and expresses emotions by making vocal sounds.
- Reaches out toward mirror image of self.

Language

- By about 4 weeks, develops distinctive cries for different situations, such as hunger or discomfort.
- Makes a variety of throaty noises, coos and chuckles.
- Next, begins to babble, vocalizing vowel sounds like "aah," "oo" and "eh."
- At around 4 months, can vocalize single syllable sounds, such as "ba," "ka," "na."
- Vocalizes instead of crying when alone.

Mental and Creative

- Within 3 or 4 months after birth, is increasingly interested in surroundings, looks around more.
- Is disturbed by angry voice.
- Watches own hand movements.
- Between 2 and 4 months, recognizes bottle or toy and anticipates excitedly by kicking legs and waving arms.
- Will turn head toward sound of rattle, looks at and reaches for toy.

- Plays with own hands, fingers and feet.
- Brings foot to mouth in exploration.
- After 5 or 6 months, nudges mother's hand or a toy to initiate movement.

Muscle Control

- When lying on back, keeps head turned to the side.
- During the first months, lifts head while lying on stomach and when held at shoulder.
- Turns body from stomach to side, then, at about 2 months, all the way over to back.
- Closes fingers around an object that is placed against palm of hand.
- Kicks legs in bicycle motion.

- Between 2 and 4 months, when lying on stomach, raises head and chest by using arms.
- Can hold a rattle for several minutes, but may drop it without noticing.
- Sits with support, holding head steady.
- Reaches for and grasps an object. If object is dangling, may try to grasp it and miss.
- Rolls over from back to stomach.

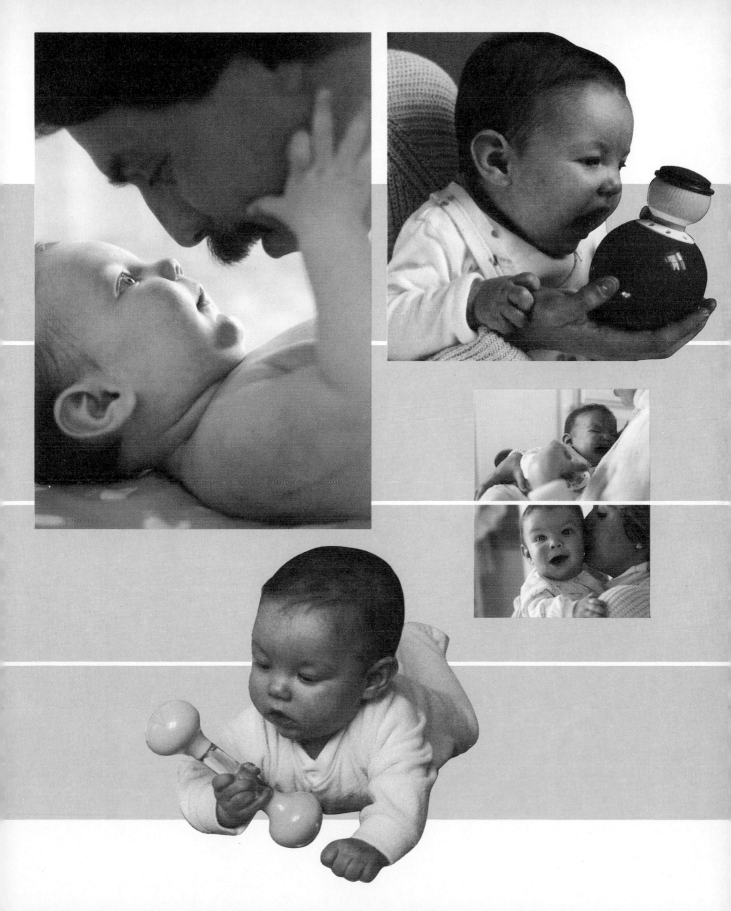

Six to 12 Months

Emotional and Social

- After 6 months of age, begins to show strong attachment to mother.
- At about 7 months, first experiences anxiety at separation from parents.
- Frowns, cries or stares when confronted by strangers.
- Smiles at and pats mirror image of self.
- By about 9 months, responds to name by turning head.
- Enjoys playing repetitive games, such as peekaboo.
- Aware of social approval, imitates amusing actions to elicit positive response.
- Begins self-feeding: Holds own bottle, eats bite-size foods with fingers, holds spoon but cannot use it.

Language

- Between 5 and 12 months, begins to vocalize double syllables, including "da-da" and "ma-ma," but these are not at first directed at parents.
- Shakes head to mean "no."
- Displays behavior that indicates understanding of some words. For instance, looks up at ceiling light fixture when parent mentions the word "light" or reaches for switch.
- Begins to imitate sounds — coughing, tongue clicking, smacking of lips.
- Sometimes stops activity if told "no."
- By about 10 months, responds to "bye-bye" by waving or vocalizing.
- Begins addressing parents as "mama" and "dada."

Mental and Creative

- Shows desire to be picked up by holding out arms.
- Plays for a couple of minutes with a toy; will bang, shake or throw it.
- If toy drops, looks for it; tries to locate hidden sounds.
- At 8 months or after, looks for family members or pets if they are named.
- Frequently reaches for objects even if hands are already full of other things.
- Purposefully uncovers object that has been hidden.
- Eager to look at pictures in book.
- Plays with a ring stack. Removes rings from spindle and randomly replaces them.
- By 10 months or so, begins simple imitative behavior — rubbing self with soap in bath, wanting to feed others.

Muscle Control

- Between 6 and 8 months of age, stands with weight on legs while held under arms or by hands. Bounces up and down while standing.
- Pulls self into a sitting position and sits without support.
- Pushes up onto hands and knees, and rocks to and fro.
- Grasps objects between thumb and forefinger.
- Around 7 or 8 months, creeps on belly, then, at about 10 months, crawls on hands and knees.
- At about 8 months, pulls up from sitting to standing while holding onto furniture, then lowers back to sitting.
- Takes object out of container and puts it back in.
- Holding onto support with one hand, stoops to pick up object from floor and stands erect again.
- At about 10 months, begins cruising — that is, walks while holding a person's hands or clinging to furniture.
- Stands alone and may take first tentative steps.

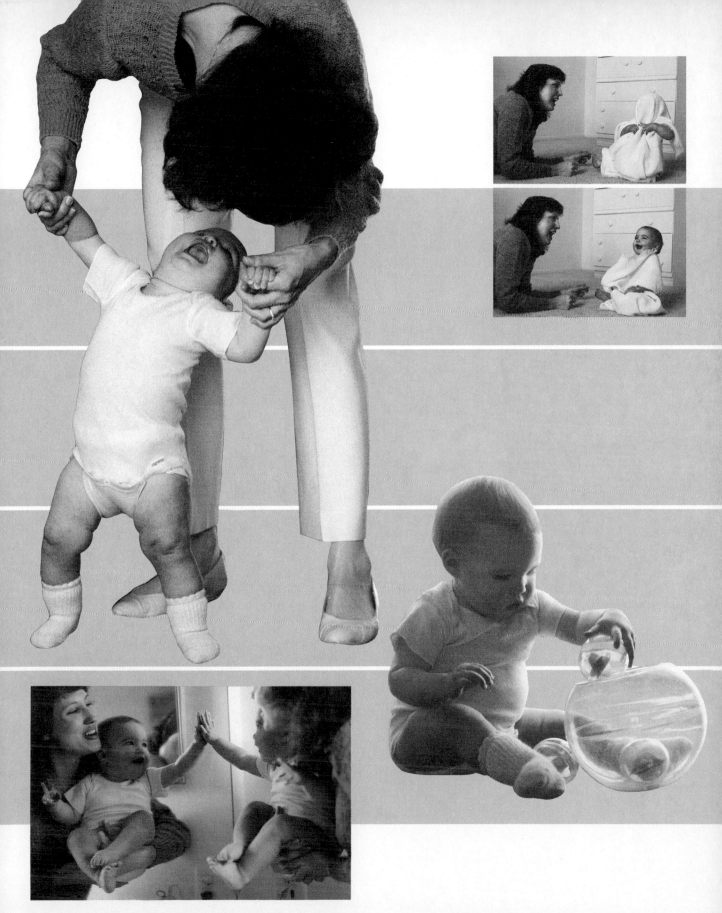

12 to 18 Months

Emotional and Social

- Early in this period, indicates desires by pointing or verbalizing; may become frustrated if not understood.
- Shows or offers toys to others.
- Kisses and hugs parents without urging.
- Displays independent behavior, acts impulsively and may resist adult control.
- Starts using a spoon to feed self — sloppily at first.
- Begins to show a sense of humor; laughs at parents' antics.
- Clearly enjoys being the center of attention.
- Expects familiar rituals and routines, especially at bedtime.
- Can remove loose clothing, such as socks or hat.
- At about 15 months of age, indicates soiled diaper by gesture or words.

Language

- Over this 6-month period, vocabulary develops from about four words, including "mama" and "dada," to 10 words or so.
- Speaks single-word sentences: "Go." "Cookie."
- Uses exclamatory expressions such as "uh-oh" and "no-no" in reaction to certain situations.
- Uses own invented words that parents may learn to understand.
- Follows simple directions: "Please give me the ball," or "Put the ball on the table."
- By 18 months, enjoys pointing to pictures in a book as adult identifies them.

Mental and Creative

- Is curious about surroundings, wants to explore and touch things. Rubs hands or mouth over interesting textures; examines sand and mud.
- Displays interest in mechanisms and moving parts; wants to see how things open and close or are put together.
- By 16 months, knows how to use certain objects, such as brush for hair and broom for sweeping. Mimics adult behavior by "helping" with housework or yardwork.
- Turns an object right side up.
- Can fit shapes into their proper openings in a three-piece shape box.
- Between 15 and 18 months, starts rudimentary make-believe behavior, such as handling a toy telephone or drinking from an empty cup.

Muscle Control

- At about 12 months, may take a few walking steps. By 14 or 15 months, walks with more confidence and runs stiffly.
- Sits down if he starts to fall.
- Climbs stairs, first by scrambling up and down on all fours, then on feet if holding an adult's hand.
- Pulls or pushes a toy while walking.
- Builds tower of two or three blocks.
- Turns book pages, although often several at a time.
- By about 16 months, throws a small ball overhand, but without much control.
- Scribbles, at first just randomly, and then deliberately repeating marks.

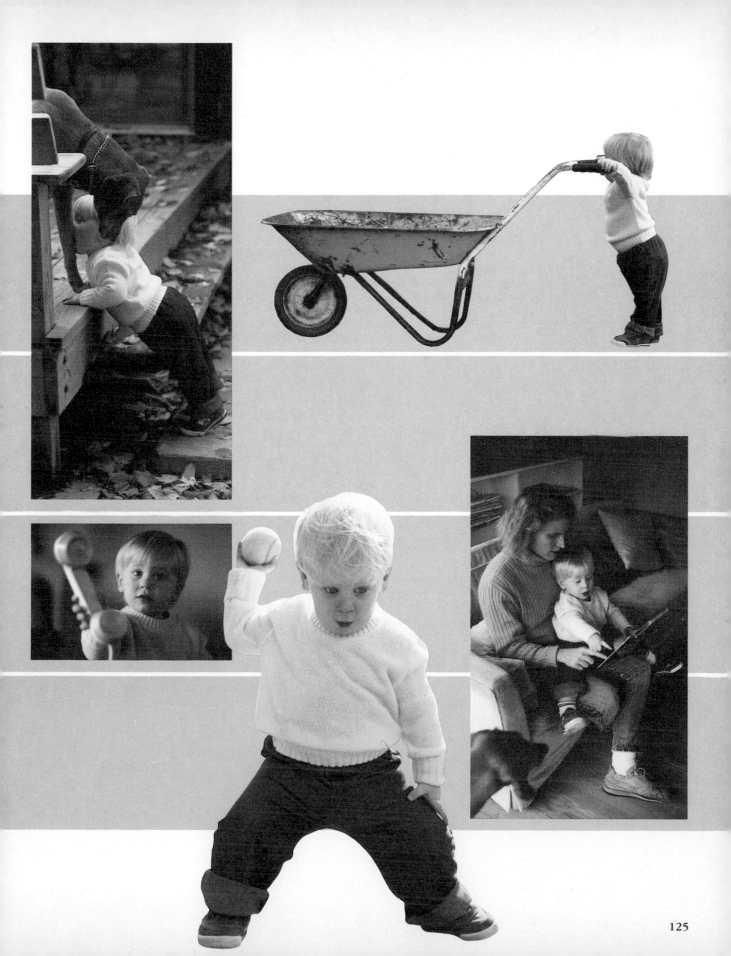

18 Months to Two Years

Emotional and Social

- During this 6-month period, expresses individuality, becomes more assertive and opinionated.
- Likely to express frustration and anger in tantrums.
- Learns about ownership of objects.
- Frequently checks whereabouts of mother, father or other caregiver.
- Shows jealousy, especially when siblings get attention.
- Enjoys playing alone and roughhousing with parent.

- Between 18 and 21 months, can remove untied shoes and unzip large zippers.
- By 24 months, puts shoes on with assistance.
- Washes and dries hands with help.
- May be ready for toilet training by 24 months.

Language

- By 20 months, uses vocabulary of about 50 words.
- Sometimes speaks in two-word phrases — "more juice," or "bye-bye car," for instance.
- Says own name when referring to self.
- Enjoys listening to nursery rhymes and music. Tries to sing songs with words.
- Loves to play labeling game, with parents naming objects when child asks, "What's that?"

Mental and Creative

- Develops ability to create mental image of object or person that is not in sight. Throughout this period, has increasing memory of past events.
- Recognizes self in photograph.
- Recognizes and points to a variety of animal pictures. May learn to imitate some animal sounds.
- By 24 months, knows about six parts of the body; points to "nose," "eyes," etc., when parent names them.

Muscle Control

- Now runs fairly well.
- Kicks a large ball by walking into it.
- Picks up toy from floor without losing balance.
- Walks backward a few steps with confidence.
- Builds tower of four to six blocks.
- Walks up and down stairs holding railing, placing both feet on a step before proceeding to the next.
- Moves body rhythmically in a simple dance.

- At about 22 months, jumps in place with both feet.
- Seats self in small chair. Climbs forward into adult chair, turns around and sits.
- Enjoys climbing around on low furniture or playground equipment.
- By 24 months, improves hand and finger agility; grasps large crayon with thumb and fingers, holds cup and uses spoon with added skill.

Two to Two and a Half Years

Emotional and Social

- Reaches peak of temper-tantrum behavior during these 6 months. Is often demanding, yet indecisive when presented with a choice. May resist parents with both words and actions.
- Begins to develop a sense of right and wrong; may stop self from reaching for a forbidden object.
- Wants to be both securely attached to parent and independent; will whine and cling but then be assertive.
- May be shy with strangers, yet aggressive toward siblings and peers — grabbing toys, refusing to share.
- May suddenly develop fears of harmless objects, such as the vacuum cleaner or the bathtub drain.
- Also notes real dangers: glass, steep stairs, big animals.
- Undresses and dresses self with assistance; pulls pants down, unbuttons large buttons. Brushes teeth with help. Uses toilet with assistance in daytime.

Language

- Uses real words more often, less gibberish.
- Speaks longer sentences, up to four words or so.
- Develops beginnings of grammar, including plurals, past tense, prepositions "on" and "in."
- By 2½ years, uses vocabulary of 275 or more words.
- Talks to self when playing.
- Listens attentively to stories and conversation.
- Likes watching television.

Mental and Creative

- Is less a creature of impulse — usually thinks before acting. Considers ideas, comes up with alternatives.
- Understands simple cause-and-effect actions: Turning a key makes the door open.
- Is more aware of time sequences. Begins using phrases like "right now," or "all done." Understands that some events happen simultaneously — for example, that mother can cook dinner while the child plays elsewhere.
- Asks many questions.
- Loves hearing familiar stories and nursery rhymes, and can occasionally join in with the words.
- Can match up shapes or basic colors. Recognizes size differences.
- Understands concepts such as "one," "many" and "another"; will ask for "another cookie."

Muscle Control

- Wants to do what adults do, such as carry large objects about. Prefers walking to being carried.
- Walks on tiptoe a few steps.
- Seats self smoothly in a chair, like an adult.
- Is typically in a hurry, running instead of walking.
- Stands on one foot momentarily before losing balance.
- Begins to jump backward and sideways while retracting arms, instead of swinging them forward.
- At about 26 months, can catch a large ball, holding arms straight in front of body, with the elbows stiff.
- By 30 months, can pedal a tricycle.
- While drawing, begins to imitate curved, vertical and horizontal lines.
- Snips around edge of paper with scissors, but not yet able to cut along a line.
- Turns pages of a book one at a time.

Two and a Half to Three Years

Emotional and Social

Emotional and Social

- Shows independence. Parts easily from mother in familiar surroundings and may refuse to hold her hand.
- Begins to obey simple rules, such as "no eating while watching television."
- Enjoys doing things for others. Gets satisfaction from helping with simple chores.
- May talk with a loud voice. Delights in giving orders.
- Can be inflexible, insisting on familiar routines.
- Participates in group games like ring-around-a-rosy under adult supervision.
- May verbally scold another child instead of being physically aggressive.
- Expands areas of self-help. Dresses with supervision. By 3 years, should be able to undress without help. Pours liquid from pitcher into glass. Uses napkin and fork. Announces need to use the toilet; may use it without help.

Language

- Gives full name if asked.
- Uses intelligible words 80 percent of the time.
- Asks "what," "where" and "when" questions.
- Enjoys being read to. May ask for a favorite book.
- Increasingly contributes to storytelling.
- Can recite simple nursery rhymes and commercial jingles with adult's help.
- May have vocabulary of 900 words by end of third year.

Mental and Creative

- Shows increased concentration, although attention span is still short.
- Expands upon pretend play, using stuffed toys, dolls.
- By about 33 months, can remember two simple directions given at once — for instance, "Get a book, then go sit where we can read a story."

Muscle Control

- By 2½ years, climbs stairs as adults do, without putting both feet on one step.
- Holds pencil with thumb and forefinger.
- Draws crude circle shape with crayon.
- Jumps from chair to floor.
- Uses scissors with greater control. Can cut paper in two, though not along a straight line.
- Kicks a ball with vigorous forward swing of the foot.

Three to Four Years

Emotional and Social

- By 3 years, is generally less tense and more secure than in the past. But until about 4 years, may regress at times, craving extra attention, bossing, behaving like a baby.
- During this year, may develop strong feelings of devotion and possessiveness to parent of opposite sex, perhaps expressing a desire to marry that parent.
- Although still very self-centered, may ask about other people's feelings.
- Enjoys a play-group atmosphere; develops friendships and begins to share.
- May acquire an imaginary friend who at times gets blamed for the child's own transgressions.
- Can do many more things for self. Puts on most clothing, having trouble only with fasteners. Holds cup by handle. Will usually stay dry overnight, but may have an occasional accident.

Language

- Improves articulation. Will mouth familiar words as an adult reads them aloud.
- Uses silly language purposely for humorous effect.
- Improvises own grammar and verb tenses — "rided" for "rode," for instance.
- May use double negatives and have trouble with irregular plurals — such as "mices" for "mice."
- Eagerly uses the telephone, listens more than speaks.

Mental and Creative

- Makes simple decisions, such as which shirt to wear.
- Holds up fingers to show age.
- Engages in dramatic play: Assumes roles, dresses for parts, uses ordinary objects as exotic props.
- Develops improved space perception. Uses some position words like "over," "beside" and "highest."
- Uses "time" — bedtime, bathtime, suppertime. Mimics adult terms such as "in a minute."
- Enjoys brush and finger painting, water and sand play, putting together jigsaw puzzles, playing with clay.

Muscle Control

- Likes to imitate adult exercises. Tries to do sit-ups, jumping jacks, somersaults.
- Runs, jumps and climbs with better coordination. By 4 years, can jump over low rope.
- Can walk a straight line heel to toe for four or five steps.
- Hops three times or so and balances briefly on one foot.

Four to Five Years

Emotional and Social

- Enters an expansive age. Grows outward emotionally; develops more self-confidence. At times, may seem almost too self-assured; may brag, refuse to follow directions.
- Is enthusiastic, willing to try and learn new things.
- Shows some courtesy to others. If taught to do so, will say "please" and "thank you" and take turns in play.
- Develops increasing interest in other children; chooses certain ones as friends.
- Is interested in where babies come from, the navel, genitals. May play "doctor" with friends.
- Can play outdoors without much supervision. Will obey simple rules: "Don't go out of the backyard."
- Is increasingly capable of caring for self. May be able to lace shoes. Can wash hands and face and brush teeth with minimal supervision.

Language

- Talks constantly. Speaking vocabulary may grow from 1,500 words at 4 years to about 2,000 or more by 5 years. Can comprehend many more words than that.
- Sometimes speaks so frankly to adults that unintentionally sounds rude.
- Wants to tell secrets and private family matters.
- Enjoys using naughty words for their shock value.
- Asks "how" and "why" questions constantly and listens closely to the answers.
- Tells elaborate stories, which are sometimes full of violence and death.

Mental and Creative

- Counts to 10 by age of 4 — probably to 30 by 5 years old.
- Begins to consider implications of own actions.
- Views the world and other people more realistically. Becomes less self-centered.
- Can match related pictures — brush to comb, ball to bat.
- Around 4½, can correctly distinguish between coins.
- Begins to understand seasons and seasonal activities. Anticipates major holidays and birthday.
- Understands size relationships between self and other objects, thus eliminating fears such as being sucked down the drain or toilet.
- Attempts to tell time by position of clock's hands.
- Pretends by emulating family roles at first, such as mother or father, and later, community roles such as carpenter or astronaut.

Muscle Control

- Learns to gallop — skipping with one foot while taking walking steps with the other.
- Carries a cup of water without spilling it.
- By 4 years, can negotiate U turns, sharp corners and obstacles on a tricycle.
- At around 4 years, draws a human as a crude stick figure or with head, eyes and legs only. Will add details such as hair and fingers by 5 years.
- Can fold paper horizontally, vertically and diagonally.
- Cuts fairly well along a line with scissors.
- Climbs trees.
- Throws a small ball with increasing skill; catches it in hands, with elbows bent.
- By 5, can print name if taught how.

Five to Six Years

Emotional and Social

- Understands the difference between acceptable and unacceptable behavior. Wants to be good, is usually eager to please — especially mother.
- Recognizes and names several emotions, fears and anxieties: "I am angry." "I'm afraid of that dog." "I don't like kindergarten."
- Is protective toward younger siblings and pets.
- Uses the social skills of giving and receiving.
- By 6 years old, in many areas can walk to school by self; crossing roads properly and safely.
- Sometimes is anxious. May bite nails, pick nose, suck thumb, wail or sulk if frustrated.
- Expands areas of self-help: Uses table knife to prepare sandwich such as peanut butter. May be able to cut soft foods with knife and fork. Can tie shoelaces if taught how. Dresses, undresses and grooms self without help.

Language

- Speaks fluently and usually uses correct grammar.
- May mispronounce words with "s" or "th" sounds.
- Tells a story using a picture book. Will memorize a favorite story.
- Loves to answer telephone and carry on a conversation. Will fetch the person the caller requests.
- Asks meanings of new words.
- Spells simple words, such as "dog," "cat," "stop," "hot."

Mental and Creative

- Is familiar with the alphabet. If taught, can read simple words in large print.
- Practices some school skills; prints name and some other letters, writes a few numbers.
- Can count small quantities and match to a numeral.
- Enjoys picture-matching games such as Old Maid.
- Understands concepts of half versus whole, bigger versus smaller.
- Uses vivid imagination in pretend play, building elaborate structures with blocks or other construction toys.
- Enjoys coloring and knows about eight colors, though cannot always answer "What color is this?"
- Distinguishes own right hand from left hand, but not the right and left hands of others.
- Can state phone number and street address.

Muscle Control

- Catches a bounced ball.
- Moves to music, approximately matching the beat.
- Has good balance. Can walk a straight line heel to toe for about 10 feet; hops on either foot for more than six steps; skips with alternate feet.
- Bends and touches toes without bending knees.
- Threads large needle and enjoys sewing with yarn through holes in a card.

Bibliography

BOOKS

Arnstein, Helene S., *What to Tell Your Child About Birth, Death, Illness, Divorce, and Other Family Crises.* New York: Pocket Books, 1964.

Atlas, Stephen L., *Parents Without Partners Handbook.* Philadelphia: Running Press, 1984.

Balter, Lawrence, *Dr. Balter's Child Sense.* New York: Simon & Schuster, Pocket Books, 1985.

Beebe, Brooke McKamy, *Tips for Toddlers.* New York: Dell, 1983.

Bowlby, John, *Attachment and Loss.* 3 vols. New York: Basic Books, 1980.

Brazelton, T. Berry, M.D.:
Infants and Mothers: Differences in Development. New York: Delta/Seymour Lawrence, 1983.
On Becoming a Family: The Growth of Attachment. New York: Delta/Seymour Lawrence, 1981.
Toddlers and Parents: A Declaration of Independence. New York: Delta, 1974.
To Listen to a Child: Understanding the Normal Problems of Growing Up. Reading, Mass.: Addison-Wesley, 1984.

Briggs, Dorothy Corkille, *Your Child's Self-Esteem.* Garden City, N.Y.: Doubleday, 1970.

Brophy, Jere E., *Child Development and Socialization.* Chicago: Science Research Associates, 1977.

Campbell, D. Ross, M.D., *How to Really Love Your Child.* New York: New American Library, 1977.

Caplan, Frank, ed.:
The First Twelve Months of Life. New York: Bantam Books, 1973.
The Parenting Advisor. Garden City, N.Y.: Doubleday, Anchor Books, 1977.

Caplan, Frank, and Theresa Caplan, *The Power of Play.* Garden City, N.Y.: Doubleday, Anchor Books, 1974.

Chess, Stella, M.D., Alexander Thomas, M.D. and Herbert G. Birch, M.D., *Your Child Is a Person.* New York: Penguin Books, 1965.

Cohen, Marilyn A., and Pamela J. Gross, *The Developmental Resource.* 2 vols. New York: Grune & Stratton, 1979.

Cole, Ann, Carolyn Haas and Betty Weinberger, *Purple Cow to the Rescue.* Boston: Little, Brown, 1982.

DeLorenzo, Lorisa, and Robert John DeLorenzo, M.D., *Total Child Care: From Birth to Age Five.* Garden City, N.Y.: Doubleday, 1982.

Dodson, Fitzhugh, *How to Parent.* New York: New American Library, 1970.

Ferber, Richard, M.D., *Solve Your Child's Sleep Problems.* New York: Simon and Schuster, 1985.

Foulkes, David, *Children's Dreams: Longitudinal Studies.* New York: John Wiley & Sons, 1982.

Fraiberg, Selma H., *The Magic Years.* New York: Charles Scribner's Sons, 1959.

Gabel, Stewart, M.D., ed., *Behavioral Problems in Childhood.* New York: Grune & Stratton, 1981.

Greenspan, Stanley I., M.D., *First Feelings.* New York: Viking, 1985.

Griffiths, Ruth, *A Study of Imagination in Early Childhood.* London: Kegan Paul, Trench, Trubner & Co., 1935.

Grollman, Earl A., ed., *Explaining Death to Children.* Boston: Beacon Press, 1969.

Hall, Elizabeth, *Child Psychology Today.* New York: Random House, 1982.

Hartley, Ruth E., and Robert M. Goldenson, *The Complete Book of Children's Play.* New York: Thomas Y. Crowell, 1963.

Hartmann, Ernest, M.D.:
The Biology of Dreaming. Springfield, Ill.: Charles C Thomas, 1967.
The Nightmare. New York: Basic Books, 1984.

Herron, R. E., and Brian Sutton-Smith, *Child's Play.* Malabar, Fla.: Robert E. Krieger, 1982.

Izard, Carroll E., *Human Emotions.* New York: Plenum Press, 1977.

Izard, Carroll E., Jerome Kagan and Robert B. Zajonc, eds., *Emotions, Cognition, and Behavior.* London: Cambridge University Press, 1984.

Jersild, Arthur T., Frances V. Markey and Catherine L. Jersild, *Children's Fears, Dreams, Wishes, Daydreams, Likes, Dislikes, Pleasant and Unpleasant Memories.* New York: Bureau of Publications, Teachers College, Columbia University, 1933.

Jones, Sandy, *Crying Baby, Sleepless Nights.* New York: Warner Books, 1983.

Kagan, Jerome:
The Growth of the Child. New York: W. W. Norton, 1978.
The Nature of the Child. New York: Basic Books, 1984.

Kagan, Jerome, and Howard A. Moss, *Birth to Maturity.* New York: John Wiley and Sons, 1962.

Kellerman, Jonathan, *Helping the Fearful Child.* New York: W. W. Norton, 1981.

Klinger, Eric, *Structure and Functions of Fantasy.* New York: John Wiley & Sons, 1971.

Leach, Penelope, *Your Baby and Child: From Birth to Age Five.* New York: Alfred A. Knopf, 1983.

Lerman, Saf, *Parent Awareness Training.* Minneapolis: Winston Press, 1980.

Levine, Melvin D., M.D., William B. Carey, M.D., Allen C. Crocker, M.D. and Ruth T. Gross, M.D., *Developmental-Behavioral Pediatrics.* Philadelphia: W. B. Saunders, 1983.

Lidz, Theodore, *The Person.* New York: Basic Books, 1968.

Millar, Susanna, *The Psychology of Play.* New York: Penguin Books, 1968.

Mussen, Paul Henry, John Janeway Conger and Jerome Kagan, *Essentials of Child Development and Personality.* New York: Harper & Row, 1980.

Mussen, Paul H., ed., *Infancy and Developmental Psychobiology.* Vol. 2 of *Handbook of Child Psychology.* New York: John Wiley & Sons, 1983.

Oppenheim, Joanne F., *Kids and Play.* New York: Ballantine Books, 1984.

Parke, Ross D., *Fathers.* Cambridge, Mass.: Harvard University Press, 1981.

Pomeranz, Virginia E., M.D., with Dodi Schultz, *The First Five Years.* New York: St. Martin's, 1984.

Pulaski, Mary Ann Spencer, *Understanding Piaget.* New York: Harper & Row, 1971.

Rubin, Richard R., and John J. Fisher III, *Your Preschooler.* New York: Macmillan, 1982.

Salk, Lee, *What Every Child Would Like His Parents to Know.* New York: Simon & Schuster, 1983.

Sarafino, Edward P., *The Fears of Childhood.* New York: Human Sciences Press, 1986.

Schaefer, Charles E., *How to Talk to Your Children about Really Important Things.* New York: Harper & Row, 1984.

Segal, Julius, and Zelda Segal, *Growing Up Smart and Happy.* New York: McGraw-Hill, 1985.

Segal, Julius, and Herbert Yahraes, *A Child's Journey.* New York: McGraw-Hill, 1978.

Singer, Jerome L., *The Child's World of Make-Believe.* New York: Academic Press, 1973.

Sparling, Joseph, and Isabelle Lewis:
Learningames for the First Three Years. New York: Berkley Books, 1979.
Learningames for Threes and Fours. New York: Walker and Co., 1984.

Spock, Benjamin, M.D., and Michael B. Rothenberg, M.D., *Baby and Child Care.* New York: Simon & Schuster, Pocket Books, 1985.

Steinhauer, Paul D., and Quentin Rae-Grant, eds., *Psychological Problems of the Child and His Family.* Toronto: Macmillan of Canada, 1977.

Sutton-Smith, Brian, and Shirley Sutton-Smith, *How to Play with Your Children (And When Not to).* New York: Hawthorn/Dutton, 1974.

Sutton-Smith, Brian, ed., *The Psychology of Play.* New York: Arno Press, 1976.

Tomlinson-Keasey, Carol, *Child's Eye View.* New York: St. Martin's, 1980.

Weiner, Irving B., and David Elkind, eds., *Readings in Child Development.* New York: John Wiley & Sons, 1972.

Wolff, Sula, *Children Under Stress.* New York: Penguin Books, 1981.

Wolman, Benjamin B., *Children's Fears.* New York: Grosset & Dunlap, 1978.

Young, Leontine, *Life Among the Giants.* New York: McGraw-Hill, 1966.

PERIODICALS

Breathnach, Sarah Ban, "Preparing for a Child's Hospitalization." *The Washington Post,* March 11, 1985.

Brent, David A., M.D., "A Death in the Family: The Pediatrician's Role." *Pediatrics,* November 1983.

Chance, Paul, "Your Child's Self-Esteem." *Parents,*

January 1982.

Cole, Joanna, "Please Don't Leave Me!" *Parents,* July 1985.

Costello, Joan, "Explaining Death to a Child." *Parents,* January 1986.

Gibson, Janice T.:
"Comforting Habits." *Parents,* February 1986.
"Raising a Toddler by Yourself." *Parents,* October 1985.

Greenspan, Stanley I., M.D., "The Best Time to Go Back to Work." *Working Mother,* November 1982.

"Hospitalizing Kids — Affects Their Siblings, Too." *Pediatrics for Parents,* October 1985.

Izard, C. E., R. R. Huebner, D. Risser, G. C. McGinnes and L. M. Dougherty, "The Young Infant's Ability to Produce Discrete Emotion Expressions." *Developmental Psychology,* January-November 1980.

Jacobs, Martha, "On the Move with Children." *Baby Talk,* August 1984.

Krucoff, Carol, "Mothers or Others." *The Washington Post,* December 18, 1985.

Lauer, Mary E., R.N., B.S.N., Raymond K. Mulhern, Jelena B. Bohne, R.N., M.S.N. and Bruce M. Camitta, M.D., "Children's Perceptions of Their Sibling's Death at Home or Hospital." *Cancer Nursing,* February 1985.

Looker, Tamsin, "The Long Goodbye: How Parents and Children Feel about Separation." *Sesame Street Parents' Newsletter,* September 1982.

Mandell, Frederick, M.D., Elizabeth H. McAnulty, R.N. and Andrew Carlson, "Unexpected Death of an Infant Sibling." *Pediatrics,* November 1983.

Nieburg, Herbert A., and Arlene C. Fisher, "When a Family Pet Dies." *Families,* April 1982.

Pomeranz, Virginia E., with Dodi Schultz, "A Brand-New Baby." *Parents,* February 1984.

Scott, Sylvia, "Your Independent Toddler." *American Baby,* November 1985.

Siegel, Benjamin S., M.D., "Helping Children Cope with Death." *American Family Practice,* March 1985.

Stirt, Joseph A., "If Your Child Needs Surgery." *Parents,* November 1985.

Strum, Charles, "Simple Answers." *The New York Times Magazine,* November 18, 1985.

Vogel, Marta, "Growing Through Grief." *The Washington Post,* February 3, 1986.

Weissbourd, Bernice:
"Coping With Separations." *Parents,* September 1983.
"I Do It Myself." *Parents,* January 1981.
"When Parents Separate." *Parents,* May 1983.
"Who's in Control?" *Parents,* December 1985.

Wessel, Morris A., M.D., "Coping with Death." *Parents,* January 1981.

OTHER PUBLICATIONS

Bayley Scales of Infant Development, "Infant Behavior Record," "Mental Scale Record Form" and "Motor Scale Record Form" New York: The Psy-

chological Corporation, 1969.

Glover, M. Elayne, Jodi L. Preminger and Anne R. Sanford, "E-LAP: The Early Learning Accomplishment Profile for Developmentally Young Children — Birth to 36 Months." Winston-Salem, N.C.: Kaplan Press, 1978.

Granger, Richard H., M.D., "Your Child From One to Six." DHEW Publication No. (OHDS) 78-30026. Washington: U.S. Department of Health, Education, and Welfare, 1978.

"HELP Chart," University of Hawaii at Manoa. Palo Alto, Calif.: VORT Corporation, 1979.

McCall, Robert B., and S. Holly Stocking, "A Summary of Research about the Effects of Divorce on Families." Boys Town, Neb.: The Boys Town Center, 1980.

"Preparing Your Child for the Hospital." Washington: Association for the Care of Children's Health, 1983.

Sanford, Anne R., and Janet G. Zelman, "LAP: The Learning Accomplishment Profile." Revised edition. Winston-Salem, N.C.: Kaplan Press, 1981.

"Talking to Children About Death." DHEW Publication No. (ADM) 79-838 Rockville, Md.: U.S. Department of Health, Education, and Welfare, 1979.

"Teaching Your Children About Sexuality." Washington: The American College of Obstetricians and Gynecologists, August 1983.

"When Parents Divorce." DHHS Publication No. (ADM) 81-1120. Rockville, Md.: U.S. Department of Health and Human Services, 1981.

Acknowledgments and Picture Credits

The index for this book was prepared by Louise Hedberg. The editors also thank: Jyotl Amin, M.D., Alexandria Hospital, Alexandria, Va.; Penny Glass, M.D., Children's Hospital, Washington, D.C.; James F. Kavanagh, Center for Research for Mothers and Children, National Institutes of Health, Bethesda, Md.; Lee McKenzie, Child Development Unit, The Children's Hospital, Boston, Mass.; Sally Provence, M.D., Yale Child Study Center, New Haven, Ct.

The sources for the photographs in this book are listed at right. They are followed by the sources for the illustrations. Credits from left to right are separated by semicolons; credits from top to bottom are separated by dashes.

Photographs. Cover: Susie Fitzhugh. 7: Bob Krist. 10: Barbara Campbell. 11: Susie Fitzhugh; Rob Johns, courtesy Joseph Campos, Psychology Department, University of Denver (2); Susie Fitzhugh — P. W. Grace/Photo Researchers. 13: Barbara Campbell. 19: Fil Hunter. 23: Barbara Campbell. 49, 58, 59: Susie Fitzhugh. 61: Suzanne Szasz. 77: Susie Fitzhugh. 79: Suzanne Szasz. 84: Fil Hunter. 89: Susie Fitzhugh. 90: Fil Hunter. 99: Suzanne Szasz/Photo Researchers. 115: Suzanne Szasz. 119-137: Susie Fitzhugh.

Illustrations. 16, 17: Kathe Scherr from photographs in *Infants and Mothers* by T. Berry Brazelton, M.D., New York: Delta/Seymour Lawrence, 1983. 18: Bobbi Tull from photograph by Fil Hunter. 24:

Kathe Scherr from photograph by Barbara Campbell. 25: Kathe Scherr from photograph by Michael Philip Manheim/Folio. 26: Kathe Scherr from photograph by Brian Lanker. 27, 28: Kathe Scherr from photograph by Fil Hunter. 29: Kathe Scherr. 30-47: Lloyd K. Townsend. 50, 51: Marguerite E. Bell. 52: Marguerite E. Bell from photographs by Suzanne Szasz. 55, 56, 64: Marguerite E. Bell. 66: Rob Wood/Stansbury, Ronsaville, Wood, Inc. 68, 69: Marguerite E. Bell. 71: Rob Wood/Stansbury, Ronsaville, Wood, Inc. 72, 73: Marguerite E. Bell. 80, 81: Rob Wood/Stansbury, Ronsaville, Wood, Inc. 84-87, 90: Bobbi Tull. 92-97: Courtesy Sylvia Feinburg. 100-109: Kathe Scherr. 111: Kathe Scherr from photograph (child) by Suzanne Szasz. 112: Kathe Scherr.

Index

experienced when person dies, 117
over parents' divorce, 110-111

H

Habits, stress-related. *See* Stress-related behavior
Hair-pulling, 62
Happy child, qualities of, 6, 8-9
Head-banging, 62
Hospital:
preparing child for stay in, 108-109
questions to ask before child enters, 109
House, childproofing, 26
Humor, developing in children, 90

I

Ideas, forming abstract, 38-44
Identification, with same-sex parent, 14, 72, 73-74, 89
Illness, hospitalization for, 108-109
Imagination:
growth of, 76, 78-79, 80, 88
role of fantasies, 88-91
sign of healthy development, 9
See also Pretend play
Imaginary friends, 76, *90,* 91
Imaginary monsters, 70, 76, 78, 82, 86, 90, *96-97*
Imitation:
behavior around 10 months, 122
of parents, by children, 14, 36-37
Independence:
asserting, by making decisions, 56
and dependent behavior, 54, 55
negative behavior and, 55-56
parents' role in encouraging, 54-55
search for, 54-57
temper tantrums and, 57
at two years, *58-59,* 64
walking and, 54, 100
Individual differences, in behavior patterns of newborns, 12-13
Infancy. *See* Babies; Newborns
Injury, fear of, 83

J

Joint custody, 112

L

Language development:
listening to young children, 28-29
stages of, 38-42, 118, *chart* 120-137
stuttering, 63
talking and reading to young children, 26
See also specific age levels
Leaving child:
with caregiver, 100-103
saying good-by, 102, 103
Limits:
internalizing, 44
setting, 9, 44, 55

Listening to children, 29
Love:
child learns about, 8
parental, 6, 8-9, 24-25, 26, 28, 29
Lying, 91

M

Make-believe. *See* Fantasies; Imagination; Pretend play
Masturbation, 72, 75
Mental development:
conceptualizing, 38-44
dreams and, 85
imagination, role of in, 88
stages of, 118, *chart* 120-137
See also specific age levels
Monsters, imaginary, 70, 76, 78, 82, 86, 90, *96-97*
Mother:
daughter's identification with, 73-74
feelings of new, 18-19
forming bond with baby, 32-34
returning to work, 100
son's attachment to, 73-74
Motor development. *See* Muscle control
Moving to a new home, 106-107
Muscle control, stages of, 118, *chart* 120-137
See also specific age levels

N

Nail-biting, 62-63
Naps, giving up, 66
"Nature versus nurture" question, 12, 13-14, 15
Negativism, 55-56
Newborns:
crying, 8, 67, 120
development, *30-32, chart* 120-121
emotional development, 18, 30-32
emotional needs of, 8, *10-11,* 18, 52
exploring senses in early weeks, 30, 31, 32
feelings of, *10-11,* 12, 18
moving to a new home, effects on, 106
personalities of, 12
scheduling differences, 12
sleep patterns and requirements, *chart* 66, 67, 84
and stepparents, 114, 115
vision of, 30, 32
waking at night, 67-68
See also Babies; Birth to six months old
Nicknames, and sensitive child, 29
Night light, 68, 82, 86
Nightmares, 73, 82, 84, 85-86, 87
Night terrors, 84, 86-87
"No" stage. *See* Negativism
Nudity, 75

O

Oedipal stage, attachment to opposite-sex parent, 73-74, 110

One-year-olds. *See* Twelve to 18 months old; Eighteen to 24 months old
Overactivity, as function of sleep problem, 67

P

Pacifier, comforted by, 60, 61
Painting, expressing feelings by, 92
Parallel play, 51
Parents:
anger of, 21, 23
attitudes toward child rearing, 18-21
children sleeping in same bed with, 68-69
coping with temper tantrums, 57
and difficult babies, 16, 17
disappointments of, 18-19
discipline styles, 28
divorced, 110-113
effect on child's personality development, 21-22
feelings and expectations, 18-22
forming bond with baby, 32-34
identification with, by children, 14, 72, 73-74, 89
imitation of, by children, 14, 36-37
meeting own needs, 22
observing behavior of newborns, 12-13, 16-17
Parent to Parent, on attitudes and feelings of, 23
reducing conflicts with child, 56
remarriage of, 114-115
saying good-by to children, 102, 103
and sex roles, 72-73
single, 113, 114-115
staying with child in hospital, 108-109
who need counseling, 20
Parents' role:
developing language skills in children, 26, 40
during toilet training, 65
encouraging independence in children, 54-55
encouraging social development in children, 50, 52-53
expressing love for their children, 6, 8-9, 25, 26, 28, 29
fostering self-esteem in children, 24-29
helping child learn to conceptualize, 38
interacting with newborns, 31, 33, 35
playing with child, 42
promoting emotional development, 6, 8-9, 10, 18, 26, 30-47
setting limits for children, 44
shaping baby's personality, 12, 13-15
teaching awareness of other people's feelings, 46
teaching organized behavior, 37
Parent to Parent:
on children's fears, 79
on parents' feelings and attitudes, 23
on stepparenting experiences, 115
on thumb-sucking, 61
Peekaboo, playing, 35, 101, 122
Permissiveness, 28
Personality:
birth order and, 15

influences on, 12-15
of newborns, 12, 13-15
parents' effect on, 21-22
siblings and, 13, 15
of twins, 12
See also Behavior
Pet, death of, 116
Piaget, Jean, 30
Picture books, 26
Play:
choosing toys, 26
evolution of, 50
judging child's maturity level by, 51
learning to share, 51, 53
parents interacting with children, 42
pretend, 9, 40, 42, 44, 45, 46, 88-90
types of, 51
See also Fantasies
Playthings:
learning to share, 53
selecting, 26
Praise, 28, 53
Preparing children for:
death of family member or pet, 116-117
divorce of parents, 110-111
hospital stay, 108-109
moving to a new home, 106-107
new baby in family, 104-105
separation from parents, 100-103
Preschooler. *See specific age levels*
Pretend play, 9, 40, 42, 44, 45, 46, 88-90
superhero phase, 80, 89
Pride, child's feeling of, 28, 52
Privacy, 75
Professional help. *See* Counseling
Pulling self up, 122
Punishment. *See* Discipline

Q
Quiet baby, 16, 17

R
Reading to children, importance of, 26
Reality, distinguishing from fantasy, 46, 88, 91
Religion, and death, 116
Remarriage of a parent, 114-115
REM sleep, 67
and dreams, 84-85, 87
Responsibility, helping child learn, 28
Risks, allowing child to take, 27
Rituals:
bedtime, 69-70, 81
burial, 116, 117
overcoming fears and anxieties by use of, 81
and security objects, 61
Rocking, rhythmic, 60, 62
Role models, for children of divorced parents, 113
Rules:
explaining reasons for, 53, 55

learning to follow, 28, 44, 52
testing behavior, 27, 55-56

S
Sadness, in baby, 10, *11*
School, fear of, 82-83
Security blanket, giving up, 61-62
Security objects, 60, 61-62
Self, developing sense of, 36-37, 54
Self-esteem:
allowing baby to explore, 25-26
child's feeling about self, 24-25, 28-29
developing self-confidence, 26-28, 54-55
development of, 24-29, 110
helping the fearful child, 83
learning to make decisions, 56-57
learning trust, 8, 9, 10, 24-25, 65, 103
parents' influence and interactions, 14, 18, 22, 24-29
self-awareness and, 36, 46, 54
sense of accomplishment, 22, 26-29, 52, 64
Senses, developing in newborn, 30, 31, 32, 33
Separation and divorce. *See* Divorce
Separation anxiety:
between six and nine months, 61, 69, 81, 100, 122
between 18 months and three years, 81-82
overcoming, 100-103
Sex education:
answering questions, 74-75
explaining differences, 72
and sexual intercourse, talking about, 75
Sex play, 75
Sex roles, 14-15
avoiding stereotypes, 72-73
experimentation with, 72-73, 89
identifying with same-sex parent, 14, 89
reinforced by parents, 14
Sexual development, 72-75
attachment to parent of opposite sex, 73-74, 110
and nudity in the home, 75
Sexual identity, 72-74, 89
and need for role models during divorce, 113
Shame, child's feeling of, 52
Sharing, learning about, 51, 53
Siblings:
birth of new baby, 104-105
influence on personality development, 13, 15
Siegel, Benjamin S., M.D., 117
Single parents, 110-115
Sitting up alone, 122
Six to 12 months old:
awareness of self as separate, 61
bedtime routines, 68, 69
developmental stages, *chart* 122-123
early attempts at communication, *34-35*
emotional development, *chart* 122-123
fear of strangers, 81
language development, *chart* 122-123

mental development, *chart* 122-123
muscle control, *chart* 122-123
separation anxiety, 61, 69, 81, 100, 122
sleep patterns and requirements, *chart* 66, 67
sleep problems, 71
social development, *chart* 122-123
Six-year-olds:
developmental stages, *chart* 136-137
sleep requirements, 66
thumb-sucking and, 60
and understanding of death, 117
Sleep:
amount required by ages, 66-67, *chart* 66
apnea, 86
children in parents' bed, 68-69
modes of, 67
naps, giving up, 66
REM, 67, 84-85, 87
See also Bedtime; Dreams
Sleep problems, 67-71
of active babies, 17
behavior related to, 67
between seven and nine months, 69
getting out of bed, 70
night terrors, 84, 86-87
of toddlers, 69-70
training child to go to sleep alone. *Expert's View* on, 71, *chart* 71
waking at night during infancy, 67-68
Sleepwalking, 70
Smiles, baby's first, 32-34
Social development, 50-53
after age five, 52
in babies, 50
between ages three and five, 51
building friendships, 53
effect of siblings on, 15
learning to share, 51, 53
parents' role in promoting, 50, 52-53
of preschooler, 9, 50
socialization process, 14, 15
stages of, *chart* 120-137
through play, 51
Standing alone, 122
Stepparents:
developing relationships with stepchildren, 114-115
Parent to Parent on, 115
Stereotypes, by gender, 15
Stimulation:
from environment, 25-26
of newborn, 13, 17, 30, 31, 32, 33
Storytelling, 90-91
Strangers, baby's fear of, 81
Stress-related behavior:
bed-wetting, 63
clinging to security objects, 60, 61-62
hair-pulling, 62
head-banging, 62